W9-CPO-922

The Story of Ernest

Copyright ©1992 Black Swan Books Ltd.
All Rights Reserved

Published by Black Swan Books
in association with the College of New Rochelle

Black Swan Books Ltd.
P.O. Box 327
Redding Ridge, CT 06876
U.S.A.

ISBN: 0-933806-65-5

The Story of Ernest

The Story of Ernest

by David Finn

Black Swan Books

For years I have wondered if I could ever write The Story of Ernest. *In one sense it seemed too elusive to be able to describe, and in another too extraordinary to be believed. I have also long felt that my knowledge of Ernest's story places a responsibility on me that I cannot shirk. With the death of Ernest's wife, Edith, on November 1, 1992, I am the only one alive today to tell the story, and if I failed to relate it on behalf of both of them, it would be an unforgivable dereliction.*

This manuscript tells the story as I know it. It is all too brief and sketchy, but perhaps it will inspire others to probe more deeply into a unique discovery which could fundamentally alter mankind's perception of the creative process.

Ernest Zierer, Berlin, circa 1930

IT WAS IN 1940 that my mother attended a series of lectures at the Metropolitan Museum of Art by Dr. Ernest Zierer, one of a growing number of German refugees who were appearing on the scene at that time. To my critical ears—at the age of nineteen—this sounded very much like an idle woman's way of attempting to acquire a little culture without trying too hard. I, of course, had never heard of Dr. Zierer and couldn't have cared less who or what he was. While the Metropolitan Museum of Art was one of the places I loved most in the world, I had avoided lecture groups like the plague. Listening to some official explanation of this or that painting or sculpture seemed the grossest violation of the profound personal experience I had when being in the presence of a great work of art. Nobody needed to tell me what to look for in El Greco's *View of Toledo*, or Brueghel's *Summer*, or Rembrandt's *Old Woman Cleaning Her Fingernails* (unfortunately for my youthful enthusiasm no longer attributed to Rembrandt). Any words spoken in explanation would be blasphemy. If you couldn't feel what was there in the painting, there was no way anyone could make you understand. I didn't tell all this to my mother, but it tainted my impression of Dr. Zierer every time she talked about all the supposedly wonderful things she was learning under his tutelage.

To my horror she announced one day that she had invited Dr. and Mrs. Zierer for dinner because she thought I would enjoy meeting them! "Be nice," she warned. "He's a fine man, and I don't want you to be rude." There was nothing I could do about it. And of course, I had no way of knowing that I was about to meet someone who I would come to believe was one of the most remarkable individuals of our time. He was relatively unknown then and is still far from being adequately recognized today; but I am now more confident than ever of the greatness of his ideas.

Instead of the know-it-all pedant whom I expected, Dr. Zierer turned out to be an extraordinarily shy man of forty-eight, almost completely bald, with warm and sensitive eyes that seemed filled with humility. He had an air of patience and inner quiet that was the exact opposite of what I had anticipated from the women's group lecturer at the Museum. Perhaps unconsciously I was also aware of the contrast between him and my father. Dr. Zierer was a man totally immersed in the private world of ideas and feelings, and totally uninterested in the world of affairs. My father was a writer who had published several books on the need for prison reform, and his interests were in how to improve the conditions of public life. Dr. Zierer's concern was what went on inside of our heads and what could make our individual lives more fulfilling. My father's concern was how people could learn to treat each other more rationally in order to achieve a more just society. They were on different wave-lengths and never were able to communicate with each other meaningfully.

In the course of the dinner, I was completely disarmed by Dr. Zierer's diffidence. He spoke in a quiet, respectful voice and with a thick German accent which seemed to make him very self-conscious. His remarks were gentle, kind, and friendly. His wife, Edith, who I later learned was fifteen years his junior (thirty-four at the time and as near to my age as his), was spritely, jovial, ebullient—an ideal counterpart to her reserved husband.

My intention had been to say nothing during the evening. They were my mother's guests, not mine. But it soon became apparent that there was something special in the way that Dr. Zierer and I related to one another. He was eager to hear all about my love of art, and listened attentively to everything I said as if I were the teacher and he the student! After dinner I offered to show my unexpectedly new-found friend what I considered to be my first serious painting. I had been drawing and painting ever since I was ten years old (when my desire to be an artist was spurred by my rejection from the art club of my elementary school because the teacher in charge said I had no talent), and a few months before I met Dr. Zierer I had begun working on a large canvas which was intended to be my inaugural statement as an adult. I also volunteered to show Dr. Zierer my favorite paintings, represented in postcard reproductions mounted inside my clothes closet where I could see them every night before going to sleep and every morning while dressing. Among them was a vigorous *Bather* by Matisse, a Memling portrait, a Rouault religious scene, a Van Eyck *Madonna and Child*, and Picasso's *Guernica*.

What, Dr. Zierer asked me gently, did I especially like about these works? "They are life itself," I said with great conviction. "You can feel the air around them, the flesh, the light, the water, the colors—all are part of a whole experience. The paintings are a world in themselves. I never tire of looking at them."

"You are right to feel as you do," Dr. Zierer said encouragingly. "But tell me about the Picasso. What do you feel about that?" I had no difficulty answering. "One of the most powerful expressions of all time. A masterpiece." Dr. Zierer's face assumed a meek expression which I learned to interpret in later years as meaning, "I understand what you are saying but I wonder if I can make clear to you that you are overlooking something essential." He tried his best in his halting Germanic English to explain. "Do you see the difference between all the other reproductions in your closet and the Picasso?" he asked. "No," I answered stubbornly. What could be different? They were all great. "But the Picasso is not a living thing, an organic thing, like the others, is it?" he asked. I was sure it was. "Look more carefully," he urged me. "It is perhaps no less great," he said, "but it is not a whole as you saw in the other paintings." His hands moved like a conductor's as if gathering the colors together to show that in the other paintings they were a cohesive whole, while in *Guernica* they were made up of isolated pieces. "In the Picasso, the black and white colors fall apart. They seem to be made of separate parts. Do you see that?" I sensed that Dr. Zierer was telling me some profound and ultimate truth about art that would make it impossible to disagree with his judgment. There was something fundamentally different between *Guernica* and all the rest. An inner quality made Picasso's depiction of death and destruction especially harrowing, precisely because it was splintered into parts, while the other paintings glowed with the richness of life. I had never been conscious of that distinction before

Then, with what I came to know as his characteristic earnestness, Dr. Zierer asked to see my new painting. I explained that it was a product of the many sketches I had made in subways or buses on the way to school, or walking the streets at night. I had created a contraption to facilitate these sketches—a medicine dropper filled with ink attached to a Chinese lettering brush, and I had filled several notebooks with quick impressions. An amalgam of those drawings, my painting was a depiction of a Salvation Army performance on a street corner. The back of a hunched-over woman playing an out-of-tune portable piano filled part of the foreground. Standing near her was a blindly devout man singing hymns to the out-of-tune musical accompaniment. A group of awestruck individuals listened to the performance as a balm for their life's struggles. I had partially painted the details of the faces of the characters and had roughly painted in the rest of the canvas. In the center was a young woman who I imagined had a beautiful spirit but was caught in the inescapable trap of poverty. I thought the prospect of salvation through the off-key street hymnals was remote. I had a story in mind for each of the figures in the painting and was sure that I had months, perhaps even years, of work ahead of me.

"It's very good," Dr. Zierer said approvingly. "So good," he added, "that you could consider it finished—just as it is. Very often, artists don't know when it's time to stop. Yet that is a very important decision to make. You should think about it." I found that a startling suggestion. It was my first experience with Dr. Zierer's way of challenging assumptions. "There is only one area that is not quite right," he said, pointing to a miscellaneous blob near the bottom of the canvas. He put his hand over the area and explained what he meant. "See how it is better if I cover up that spot," he said. He took his hand away, and then put it back, and to my amazement I could see that when he removed his hand there was indeed something wrong with the painting. How could he know? I wondered. And what was the nature of the problem? "What should I do?" I asked. "Is the color wrong? Is it too dark?" "Not at all," he said gently. "It is simply a break in the painting. Just paint over it, using the same color if you'd like, and you'll see, it will be better."

That was my introduction to what Dr. Zierer later referred to as "Non-Associative Art Evaluation," or "Absolute Art Evaluation." I couldn't wait to paint over that area and did so the next day. As predicted, the problem he had shown me the previous evening disappeared with a few brushstrokes. And although I was a little disoriented that my painting could be considered finished when I thought I had barely started, I was stimulated by the opportunity to begin a new canvas. I also felt that Dr. Zierer had demonstrated an uncanny sense of what made a painting "right" or "wrong" without ever letting his personal tastes interfere.

A few days after our first encounter I telephoned Dr. Zierer to ask if I could come to see him. He lived in a walk-up on West 152nd Street, which was convenient for me since I was going to City College, only a few blocks away. His wife was away during the day working in what she described as a sewing factory while he looked for a permanent job at a university. When I arrived at their tiny apartment, he was doing the ironing and cooking supper. We spent the afternoon talking about art, and I felt a whole world opening up for me.

The revelation—and that is not too strong a word—began when Dr. Zierer showed me a series of paintings by artists who had been students of his in Berlin. To begin with, he showed me a painting of a still life. He said that whenever we look at a painting we associate the subject with things we know. We recognize a bowl, flowers, a table, and the shapes of those familiar objects determine what we customarily refer to as "composition." Our attitudes towards the colors, the painting technique and, of course, the style of the painting are affected by this associative reaction to the painting. Even in an abstract painting we recognize geometric elements or variously shaped color areas based on an associative response to the forms. These are the building blocks of traditional aesthetic judgments. All of this, however, was irrelevant to what he wanted me to see in a painting.

If one looks at a painting in a non-associative way, Dr. Zierer explained, the way someone who had no contact with human culture as we know it might see it, all that could be identified would be color particles. In an article he and Mrs. Zierer wrote some years later ("Leonardo da Vinci's Artistic Productivity and Creative Sterility," *The American Imago*, vol. 14, no. 4, [Winter 1957]), the idea of "color particles" was explained in some detail. "Each color in any painting," it states, "is actually a composite of innumerable color particles, to which every brushstroke, the strength, direction and manner of application, gives further shadings. The aggregated qualities which determine such a color particle interrelation cannot be conveyed of course by a mere enumeration of color masses." In other words, "color particles" are not areas of color as in a "blue" sky, or a "green" field, or a "red" barn, but rather the atomic make-up of a painted area, consisting of vast numbers of tiny particles of color which can have a bond to each other comparable to a magnetic force. Our judgment of the painting would thus not be in terms of what we liked or disliked, which ultimately was a matter of taste— even with sophisticated art historians or critics; it would be in terms of what was objectively there in the painting itself. Hence his use of the terms "non-associative" and "absolute." What we would discover in the paintings was not a "relative" quality based on personal feelings, but objective judgments which could be made equally by all people.

To explain what he meant, he told me the story of an anthropologist who wanted to record the music of a certain primitive tribe. He wrote the notes for the melody of one of the pieces of music being performed for a ritual dance, but was surprised to discover it to be entirely different when it was repeated. In fact, every time the members of the tribe performed this piece of music, it had a different melody. He finally realized that what was the same was the rhythm, which they considered to be the basic element of the music. The melody was at best incidental. What he associated with the sound was completely different from what they associated. The only way he could hear the music the way they heard it was to put out of his mind entirely all the associations he brought to the act of listening and to pay attention to the aural impulses—as discrete sounds—that reached his ears. This was the non-associative and absolute reality of the music, independent of personal or cultural reactions.

Dr. Zierer then turned the painting upside down and took out a second painting, which he also turned upside down, for purposes of comparison. He said he wanted me to look at the paintings just as collections of color elements, without bringing any associations to them. He wanted me to look at what was there in the painting itself; not at what I would tend to see on the basis of my accumulated knowledge. Focusing on that kind of response, he showed me one painting which he called "organic" and another which he called "inorganic." He later changed these terms to "integrated" and "disintegrated" and I will use those words here to avoid confusion. To draw my attention to what he was talking about, he said he would give me some circumscriptions. They couldn't be descriptions since words were in themselves associations. These phrases would help me understand what it was that he was referring to. The following is my recollection of his circumscriptions:

In the "integrated" painting—as he and I had discussed when looking at my postcard reproductions—the colors seem to flow into each other; there is something like a magnetic force holding the painting together as a single unit; everything belongs together; one feels as if one can sink into the painting; the colors seem alive.

In the "disintegrated" painting—as he had told me about Picasso's *Guernica*—the colors seem to fall apart; they look as if they could be cut out and pasted together; the painting seems to consist of separate pieces; there seems to be no magnetic force binding the color particles together; the colors seem dead; "the colors fight each other"—a phrase which my oldest daughter used many years later, and which Dr. Zierer especially liked.

What Dr. Zierer showed me seemed perfectly clear. Then he brought out several more paintings,

Fig. A: Integrated

14

Fig. B: Disintegrated

some integrated and some disintegrated. In every case, I could easily identify which each one was. And I realized that each painting was selected in order to demonstrate a different point. One might think that integrated paintings had harmonious colors which gave the impression of blending together; he showed me one that had discordant colors that was clearly integrated and one with harmonious colors that was disintegrated. The same was true of paintings with hard edges, paintings with strongly contrasting light and dark areas, paintings with an impasto technique. None of these characteristics would determine whether a painting was "integrated" or "disintegrated," as Dr. Zierer used those terms.

Color reproductions of paintings, Dr. Zierer explained, might not show whether the original paintings were integrated or disintegrated because color nuances could change in the printing process. He said that reproductions of black-and-white paintings would be more reliable, and to illustrate this point for this book, I have created a series of paintings to help readers understand what he was talking about (Figs. A,B,C,D,E,F,G,H,I,J). In creating these paintings, I recall several other distinctions Dr. Zierer pointed out. One was that in a disintegrated painting, where there may be a number of tonal areas that are separated from each other, one feels almost as if one could count them; in an integrated painting, the tonal areas blend into the whole. If there are lines in an integrated painting, the lines seem to be an integral part of the spaces that are painted around them. In a disintegrated painting, the lines seem more like a decoration. A disintegrated painting may have a spritely, poster-like quality that catches the eye and has an immediate appeal; while in an integrated painting of the same subject, the tones appear to have depth and richness which invite the eye into the surfaces. In a disintegrated painting, the elements seem to stand out as separate objects; while in an integrated painting, they all seem part of the whole. What accounts for the difference remains elusive, although it seems so obvious when it is pointed out. In black-and-white paintings, one thinks that the integrated paintings are simply more "painterly," while the disintegrated paintings are like designs; but it is the integration in the painting which gives it that painterly quality and the disintegration which gives it a design quality. The question is, what makes something integrated or disintegrated?

"The unconscious energy within you," Dr. Zierer explained during that first conversation at his apartment, "produces one result or the other. It is an unconscious process. The result is evident in the way the color particles are related. In one case, there is a magnetic force binding the particles together; in the other case, that force is missing and the particles are disconnected. One paints an integrated or disintegrated painting, depending on what is going on in one's unconscious mind at the time the painting is being done. It is like life. If you feel that everything in your life is flowing together and part of a living continuity, it will be evident in your painting, which will be integrated. If you feel a disconnectedness between the experiences of your life, your painting will be disintegrated." Integrated and disintegrated states are not a continuum, any more than living and not living. They are two discrete and entirely different states of being.

It was hard to believe. But to demonstrate his

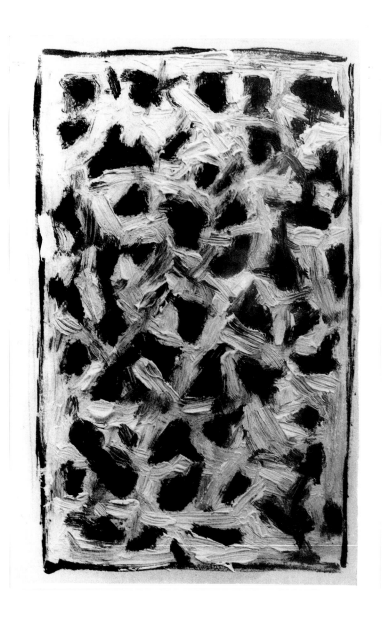

Fig. C: Integrated

Fig. D: Disintegrated

Fig. E: Integrated

Fig. F: Disintegrated

21

point he asked me to paint an integrated painting, which I did without giving the project much thought. I made no conscious effort to paint an integrated painting; my mind was simply prepared to respond. I couldn't tell how or why; it just came out that way. Every part of the integrated painting was integrated; it could have been cut apart into arbitrary sections and each section would be integrated. After several tries, I learned that if one area of an integrated painting turned out to be disintegrated (usually by happenstance and without significance), the "break," as Dr. Zierer called it, could be "solved" by painting over it, even with the same colors. That was what Dr. Zierer had noticed in my Salvation Army painting and it had been easily corrected.

It seemed to me that integrated paintings were visible expressions of what Henri Bergson called the *élan vital*, and that they were "better" than disintegrated paintings. To my surprise, Dr. Zierer was hesitant to make that distinction. It was true, he said, that virtually all the great paintings that had survived through the ages were integrated. But we must recognize, he said, that death is as real as life. It was clear that he had originally chosen the word *organic* because it had to do with life and the word *inorganic* because it had to do with death or inanimate things. But could one say that one was better than another? With my passionate preference for life, I could see no reason why not. But for reasons I could not quite understand, Dr. Zierer insisted on being dispassionate. He said emphatically that there are many integrated paintings which he didn't like and many disintegrated paintings that he did like. "Like and dislike have nothing to do with integrated and disinte-

grated," he said. He did point out, however, that disintegrated paintings were well suited for commercial art, where it was important to communicate a quick message, because disintegrated works were striking, eye-catching, attention-getting. Integrated paintings were quieter, deeper, more enduring. But as he had explained in our first conversation, he could consider Picasso's *Guernica* a great painting, even though it was disintegrated. The nature of its calamitous subject was quite understandably accompanied by an unconscious state of mind which produced a disintegrated painting, and this fact contributed to the power of the work.

This was the first of many doors opened into Dr. Zierer's theory. The second door was opened on my next visit a few days later. This time he introduced me to his concept of tension. (He later changed the term tension to color intensity because he thought tension—which was a translation of the German *Spannung*—had an unpleasant connotation in English. But to me, tension suggested tensile strength which is close to what he meant.) A painting (integrated or disintegrated) could have a greater or lesser tension, and the capacity of an artist to achieve a greater—or higher—tension was a measure of his talent (or as he later called it, his integrative capacity).

The higher the tension, the more powerful or greater the painting seemed; the lower the tension, the less important it seemed. Artists strive to paint on an ever increasing level of tension, Dr. Zierer explained. If an artist overreached himself and tried to achieve a tension that was beyond his or her personal limits, the painting would be disintegrated.

There were three ways in which one could

Fig. G: Integrated

Fig. H: Disintegrated

Fig. I: Integrated

Fig. J: Disintegrated

increase the tension of a painting, and in this regard Dr. Zierer said he could describe the techniques of how to produce the desired result through a conscious effort (unlike integration and disintegration which are the result of unconscious processes).

These techniques were:

Increase the size of a color area. A surface divided in half with one color in each area would have the highest tension. It would be virtually impossible for anyone to produce an integrated work at this level.

Increase the contrast of colors on a tension spectrum—a special spectrum discovered in this connection. In it, yellow and purple would yield a higher tension than blue and green, and the greatest tension would be between black and white.

Achieve what he called reduction. This was the most complicated. A color would be affected by surrounding colors, or shadings within the color area—even those caused by the way light was reflected on brushstrokes. The same color in different parts of a painting might look different, depending on the colors around it, the size of the area, and the way it was painted. But if two or more parts of a painting had the same visual color effect, the result would be the same as if they were part of the same color area. This would mean that the color area would be enlarged and the tension increased.

Because of reduction, a simple checkerboard in which each square is the same and each of the two colors the same, all painted flat, geometrically exact and hard-edged, would have the same tension as a surface divided evenly into two colors.

To raise the tension of one's painting, one should keep all three techniques in mind. In a gallery or museum, when you find that one painting seems stronger or more important or bigger than other paintings of the same size and style, you can usually tell which of the three techniques have been used to raise the tension. Thus, if one looked at two paintings by a particular artist, and one was clearly of a higher tension than the other, although both had roughly the same colors and used the same painting technique, the painting with the higher tension would have succeeded in achieving that result either because of greater contrast, larger flat areas of paint, or the subtle reduction of the colors through skillful brush work.

I have painted two versions in black and white of a simple subject — a house, a road, bordered by trees and a sky — to show the difference between low and high tension. The painting with the higher tension seems stronger, more vigorous and more important than the one with the lower tension. Both paintings are integrated (Fig. K and L).

Dr. Zierer later developed fourteen different levels of tension and was able to identify a painting as being on one level or another. In effect, he created a scale by selecting fourteen paintings that had different degrees of tension. At one end of the scale was a painting with the weakest or lowest tension. At the other end was a painting with the strongest or highest level. Incremental differences were represented by the other paintings between the two extremes. These fourteen paintings became standards, and when Dr. Zierer wanted to determine the level of a new painting, he would hold it up to the standards and match it up to the tension level which seemed to correspond to it most closely. The lower levels were

Fig. K: Lower Tension

Fig. L: Higher Tension

A, A-1 to A-7. The higher levels were B, B-1 to B-5, with B-5 the highest. Levels A and B-5 were the two extremes which were only theoretical and virtually non-existent. I never asked him why he chose an A and B grouping instead of just numbering the scale from 1 to 14, but I assumed that he thought the dividing line between the two categories was significant, with the A levels representing a severely repressed personality and the B levels representing a "normal" personality. Artists could improve their work by striving always to paint at the highest possible tension. Dr. Zierer said that the real measure of what might be called one's talent was the level of tension one was capable of achieving in an integrated painting. This potential could also be called one's creative capacity. It was for that reason that Dr. Zierer called his theory a method of "art evaluation" rather than "art criticism." The higher the level, the higher the value.

As an exercise to test one's capacity, one could undertake the challenge of doing a checkerboard painting, and by modifying the colors slightly with shadings or different pigment effects (thicker and thinner brushstrokes), and with modifications of the size or evenness of the squares, one could produce an integrated painting at a relatively high tension. In fact, Dr. Zierer hypothesized that doing a checkerboard painting might indicate the highest potential of one's creative capacity. (Mrs. Zierer told me that Dr. Zierer later abandoned the idea that people had fixed limits to their creative capacity. Higher levels could be reached in old age than ever before, and there was no way to determine an ultimate potentiality. As I grew older I found that a much more agreeable theory!)

The notion of being able to produce increasingly important paintings by working hard to achieve a higher tension proved to be a tremendous stimulus to my youthful artistic ambition. In the days and weeks that followed, I turned out painting after painting for Dr. Zierer to evaluate and I felt that I was making tremendous progress.

There was another important aspect of painting, Dr. Zierer explained, and that was the artist's individuality. Each of us, he pointed out, would do our best work if we found the style or underlying idea in our creative work that was a manifestation of our own particular way. The style or idea which we developed might not be of special importance in judging a painting's essential qualities; that would be determined by whether it was integrated or disintegrated and what its level of tension was. But finding one's own individual way was a vital step in an artist's personal development. And when that step was taken, the capacity to achieve higher tension would be enhanced. It was as if discovering a way to express one's personal vision would release the creative energies within one's unconscious being. (I later remembered the importance of that idea when, looking at some early Van Gogh paintings, I realized that although they were important historically, they were on a much lower level than his later work and gave no indication of the tremendous latent energy which would burst forth when the mature artist had found his uniquely personal way to express himself.)

As my paintings proliferated, I wondered how my personal way might develop until one day Dr. Zierer volunteered the suggestion that I was moving in the direction of finding a new form of lightness in my work. He pointed to Monet's paintings as having achieved a quality of lightness that had not existed before and speculated that I might be able to discover a new stage in that progression. This was exciting to me, and as I painted more and more furiously, I began to see how developing one's own style could be a factor in achieving greater tension. As the weeks went by, I would trot up to Dr. Zierer's apartment with a canvas in tow, often while the paint was still wet, to get his judgment as to the tension I had been able to achieve. Occasionally he would show me a disintegrated break in a painting by covering over an area with his hand to show me that something was wrong. I always could see what he meant and found that when I solved that problem, the painting was substantially improved. Also, from time to time, Dr. Zierer pointed out one area of a painting that had a lower tension than the rest, and I would work on that area to improve it.

The third door of Dr. Zierer's theory opened when he introduced me to what he called intuitive paintings. He said there were not two but three categories of painting—organic, inorganic, and intuitive. Intuitive was the supreme quality in a work of art. In an intuitive painting, the colors were not "bound" to each other as was the case with integrated paintings, nor were they separated from each other as with disintegrated paintings. The colors were both connected and free. When one looked at an intuitive painting one felt as if one were floating in the painting. Intuitive paintings were in another sphere, a world of their own, unlike integrated paintings which were of this world. Dr. Zierer showed me an intuitive painting he had done himself, and I could tell that the colors seemed to be in a different space. Later I was able to recognize an intuitive painting as one that seemed to glow with an inner light. It was of a different order from integrated paintings. I saw this most dramatically with the two *Sunflower* paintings by Van Gogh at the Tate Gallery in London; they were almost identical in subject matter, color, composition and technique, yet one was vastly different from the other; one glowing as if in a higher realm of existence because it was intuitive, and the other settled in its "normal" environment because it was integrated. I subsequently found this to be the case with other Van Gogh paintings which were identical in every respect, except that one was intuitive and seemed to jump out of its frame, and the other was integrated and was contained within the frame.

(Many years later Dr. Zierer told me to my dismay that he had dropped the concept of intuitive as a separate category, and that he considered such paintings as integrated but on a very high level. Since I continued to see—and do to this day—a distinctly different character in intuitive paintings, I did not respond to his new thought and we agreed to disagree. I suspected he dropped the category only because it had no relevance to his later work in the field of psychology, but I was sure it retained its validity in the field of art.)

Dr. Zierer explained to me that his entire theory had begun with his discovery of intuitive paintings. Years ago, he said, when looking at a painting in the Prado Museum, he became aware of a quality in the painting that he had experienced in another painting in another gallery of the museum. He went back and forth, studying the two paintings, trying to understand what that remarkable quality was. When he felt he had recognized the characteristics, he undertook a methodical search through the museums of Europe, to identify all the paintings that had this special quality which he decided to call "intuitive." That taught him to look at paintings in a certain way, free of the associations which formed the basis for other forms of art criticism. With that new insight, he was able to identify what he decided to call integrated and disintegrated, and so his theory was born. (Dr. Zierer always called it his "theory," although the more I learned about it and saw for myself the incontrovertible evidence that what he declared about various paintings was a "reality," not a "theory," I came to think of it increasingly as Dr. Zierer's "discovery.")

Not long after I learned about intuitive paintings, Dr. Zierer took me on a tour of both the Museum of Modern Art and the Metropolitan Museum of Art to point out examples of the categories he had been talking about, and it was almost as if I'd never seen those galleries before. At the Museum of Modern Art, I remember a surrealist painting by Peter Blume—called "The Eternal City," with a jack-in-the-box portrait of Mussolini—that Dr. Zierer pointed out as being intuitive. At the Metropolitan, he showed me that Raphael's impressive painting *The Madonna and Child Enthroned with Saints* was integrated, while his small painting *The Agony in the Garden*, shown nearby, was intuitive. (John Pope-Hennessy may have experienced this same quality about the latter when he wrote in his book on Raphael that *The Agony in the Garden* had "an inwardness and privacy no Umbrian painting of the theme had had before." [*Raphael*, New York University Press, 1970, p. 136]) Another significant observation was that *The Birth of the Virgin* by Fra

Carnevale was completely disintegrated ("completely" meaning that there was no part of the painting that was integrated). I was a little startled to realize that a painting which had survived for 500 years and was considered one of the treasures of the Metropolitan Museum was disintegrated, but Dr. Zierer stuck to his guns, explaining that there was no reason why a disintegrated painting could not be important in the history of art.

Following our visit to the Metropolitan, I did my best to put myself in a state of mind to paint an intuitive painting, but to my chagrin failed to achieve my goal. I was able to produce integrated paintings at increasingly high levels, but I never succeeded in creating an intuitive painting. I considered this a telltale mark of my inadequacy, but Dr. Zierer did not. Rembrandt, Goya, Cézanne were great artists, he pointed out, and may not ever have painted an intuitive work. As the years went by, I became more and more conscious of the supreme greatness of intuitive works when I came across them in a museum; but I accepted Dr. Zierer's judgment that the failure to produce an intuitive work was not anything to be ashamed of.

A significant moment came in my life when I gathered up enough courage to ask Dr. Zierer if I could call him by his first name, Ernst (later Americanized to Ernest). "Of course," he said smilingly, and explained that in the European tradition when an older person called a younger person by his first name, as he had been calling me by mine, the younger person could take that as an invitation to call the older person by his first name. Somewhat after that, we became fast friends, despite the thirty-year difference between us.

My visits to Ernest and Edith's apartment (my permission to use first names extended to Mrs. Zierer as well) became more frequent. When I would arrive there after school, I would often find Ernest typing slowly at his desk, usually a letter to one or another university inquiring about a possible teaching position in the art history department. He would stop his work and turn to ironing clothes or preparing dinner, chores he could do while talking to me. Sometimes I would stay there until Edith came home, and the three of us would have dinner together. They would talk about their childhood—Edith explaining how she had met Ernest when she was fifteen and fell in love with him, how close she had been to her family (all of whom died in concentration camps), how she and Ernest had managed to escape to Sweden from Germany and later come to the United States with virtually no possessions. It was from Edith that I learned about the Zierer School in Berlin of which she had been especially proud. It was an institution in which Ernest's theories were taught to painters, writers and musicians—since the same categories existed in all the arts. One of the interested visitors to the school had been the famous pianist Claudio Arrau, who came to many discussions and lectures. Kandinsky had also learned something about his theory and invited Ernest to visit his studio and comment on some paintings that he was working on. Ernest pointed out a disintegrated break in what was otherwise an integrated painting and explained that the painting would be improved if Kandinsky worked some more in that area. The artist was grateful, according to Ernest, because he had felt there was something wrong with that painting but couldn't figure out what the problem was. Kandinsky was sure that Ernest's analysis was correct and reworked the painting. (I had a similar experience some years later when I pointed out to my friend Henry Moore that a section of one of his sculptures [called *Torso* (1967)] seemed "to stick out" and not be an "integral part" of the rest. Moore's reaction was very much like Kandinsky's. Although it was most unusual for him to change a sculpture because of a critical comment, and this one had already been cast in bronze, Moore said he would remove the troublesome part. Some time later I learned that he had done just that. He kept the one cast of the original plaster as an "artist's copy," and no further casts were made. Then he modified the plaster by cutting off the part that was a disintegrated break and made a new series of casts of the revised work.)

It was Edith who also told me that Ernest had completed an encyclopaedic book describing in detail all aspects of his theory and identifying works of art in European museums that fell into the various categories he had worked out. He had written several books before that, but this was to be his master reference work. Unfortunately, the book was being printed when the Zierers received word that they had to leave Germany. One copy of the manuscript was left with Edith's parents but was lost in the Holocaust. A second copy was destroyed in a flood that inundated Ernest's office files some years later. The plates for the book had already been made by the publisher, but these too had apparently been destroyed. To compound the problem, Ernest was having a hard time mastering English, and it was going to be very difficult for him to present his ideas in a language that was foreign to him. Producing that book—or a book which would enable future generations to understand Ernest's theory—became something of an obsession, particularly for Edith and me, which we struggled with for over forty years.

When the Zierers came to the United States, cousins of theirs who lived in New York were helpful to them, but they had few friends. They had never considered having children because of their problems in Germany and their struggles in America. And I knew that as we grew closer, I was becoming a member of their family, as well as one of a devoted circle of artists who had been Ernest's followers both in Germany and in Sweden—a group of artists who embraced Ernest's theory as warmly as I had.

The most outstanding and closest of these friends was Johann Walter-Kurau—a Russian born *emigré* artist in Germany who, although older than Ernest, had been his star pupil. He was a widely recognized artist at the time and his works were in a number of museum and private collections. Ernest had written a book about his work in German, which although I was able to look at, since I knew no German, could not read. I felt that the distinctions of integrated and disintegrated paintings, as well as levels of tension, seemed to be evident in the illustrations (I do not think Walter-Kurau ever produced an intuitive painting). Ernest also told me about Walter-Kurau's idea to reverse the light and shadow patterns of the world around him, painting the dark areas light and the light areas dark. This produced a vigorous style which was quite distinctive and impressive. The only possessions of value which the Zierers brought out of

Germany with them were twenty or thirty rolled-up Walter-Kurau canvases, along with canvases by other painters in the Zierer school, such as Oscar Gavell, Theodore Ortner, and Peter Paul Fechner. Later Edith gave me some of the Walter-Kurau paintings, and I in turn gave some of them to the Guggenheim and other museums that felt they were an important part of the Berlin art scene in the twenties and thirties.

As time went on, I learned about more aspects of Ernest's theory. He told me, for instance, that there were two sub-categories of integrated paintings—one qualitative and one quantitative. The qualitative was what one saw in most integrated paintings, but the quantitative had the appearance of a more superficial painting. The colors still flowed together, but they seemed to be more on the surface; one didn't quite have the same feeling of depth. Every now and then I would unwittingly produce a painting that was an example of quantitative organism, and even before Ernest pointed it out to me, I knew what was wrong. The trouble was that once in the quantitative groove, so to speak, I could not consciously change it to qualitative organism. I had to put the painting away and come back to it another time, or just move on to another canvas.

We also talked about line drawings, and Ernest explained to me that what was important, in relation to integration and disintegration, was the spaces around the lines, created, as it were, by the gradations of the lines themselves. We looked at many drawings together, and when they were integrated, I could feel the whole surface of the area come alive, just as surely as if I were looking at a painting.

The analysis of line drawings was later mentioned

in the article by the Zierers on Leonardo da Vinci:

> . . . the "modulated" line-drawing has all the possibilities of creative expression; it is, in a way a condensed achromatic painting. A thickening or roughening in one part of the line, lightness of touch in the other, gives the impression of an "invisible modeling" to the outline, which in turn gives the enclosed unpainted area the achromatic shadings and nuances, the—imperceptible—color elements which are decisive . . .

As I was very interested in literature also (I was an English major in City College), we talked about writing as well. Poetry, Ernest said, was like line drawings, and one had to feel the binding together (or its lack) in the areas around the words. I tried to read some poetry with him to get his judgment about different works, but he said that his understanding of English was too limited. He did tell me about certain German authors who produced integrated novels at a very high level, Jacob Wasserman being one of the most outstanding. I had never heard of Wasserman, but managed to buy a good many of his works translated into English and found them to be extraordinarily powerful. *Caspar Hauser*, Ernest said, was one of the "strongest" (meaning highest in tension) of Wasserman's works. *The Gooseman*, he said, was intuitive. Ernest said he couldn't speak for the English version of the novels, but when I read them I thought they were superb. Ernest was not inclined to read novels or poetry in English, probably because of his difficulty with the language, but Edith read incessantly. She devoured almost any novel she could find in the library, and she constantly told me about books she read that were integrated and were on a high level of tension—a judgment I felt to be very dependable. We even talked about films, and I remember that Ernest and Edith said that a film based on a William Saroyan play, *The Time of Your Life*, was integrated.

The more I learned about Ernest's ideas, the more aware I became that evaluating a painting in terms of his theory required a critical judgment, and that the ultimate judge was Ernest himself. I had no doubt about my own ability to make basic distinctions, and I could see that Edith was at least equally confident of herself. On finer distinctions I would have to check with Ernest in order to be sure. This was most clearly evident when we discussed disintegrated breaks in paintings. I might feel there was something wrong in a particular area, but often I would think the problem was in one daub of color, when Ernest would demonstrate, with his hand over an adjacent part, that I had picked the wrong spot. There was never any doubt that he was right once he had pointed it out, but I knew that his "feel" was the only resource that could be absolutely relied on. Every now and then I would make a bad mistake, but he was too kind and sensitive to tell me outright. His countenance would change to a pained expression which I could always recognize, and he would try to tell me as gently as possible why I was wrong. But when I was right, which happily was nine times out of ten, he was obviously very pleased, and spoke to me as if I were a graduate student and had mastered my subject admirably.

One day Ernest told me about his theory of stages of history. It was not until much later that I became familiar with other cyclical views of history, but I felt then—and still feel—that his periodic theory was more of a discovery than a theory. It seemed factual rather than speculative, and was based on hard evidence that one could see with one's eyes. There were seven basic periods, he explained, and they could be represented by symbols. The first was symbolized by the point; this could be seen, for instance, in the era following the fall of the Roman empire. The Merovingian period was roughly equivalent to the horizontal, Romanesque to the circle, Gothic and early Renaissance to the vertical, the late Renaissance to the ellipse, the Baroque to the diagonal, and the contemporary to the spiral. Ernest also said that the earliest of these periods was the "darkest," and that as each new era came into being, it became distinctively "lighter." He meant "dark" and "light" as being a psychological experience rather than merely an optical phenomenon. He could determine, he said, by the darkness or lightness of a work of art which period it was painted in, and he was as confident about that determination as he was of levels of tension. We spoke briefly about other cultures, and he believed that all cultures around the world were subject to the same periodicity.

Ernest did not make an effort to elaborate on the historical accuracy of his concept; it was an observation he thought worth noting, and had even written a small book about it (in which he had suggested that the seven periods might find a parallel in astronomy, with the earth, for instance, being subjected to seven different motions or pulls—an idea which I thought was going too far). He also told me that when the *Mona Lisa* was stolen from the Louvre and then recovered, he was one of the experts called upon to determine whether the returned painting was authentic. He was able "unequivocally" to state that it was— first because it was intuitive, and a copyist could not have reproduced the intuitive quality, no matter how accurate a copy it was; and secondly, because he could tell by the level of "darkness" or "weight" of the painting that it was done in the "oval" era (which would not have been the case with a twentieth century copy). As another illustration of his idea, he pointed out that paintings in the middle of the nineteenth century became lighter—with brighter colors and with an airiness that was substantively different from the previous period. The same quality of whiteness, or lightness, continued into the twentieth century. Later, Abstract Expressionists such as Jackson Pollack gave direct evidence of the importance of the spiral motif in their work. Although we didn't discuss it, my guess is that Ernest would have detected the same inner lightness in Ad Reinhardt's black paintings as in Richard Pousette-Dart's white paintings. The colors were as black as could be in the former, but it was a different kind of darkness from that found in Byzantine or medieval paintings, which were not only dark but "heavy."

During our discussions, I wondered if in our time we were nearing the end of the "spiral" era, and I asked Ernest how he thought we would revert to the "point" era, and what would happen to the world when that took place. He said he had no idea, but that the transition had taken place many times before in the course of time, and somehow it would happen again. I pointed out that there seemed to be a growing tendency towards disintegrated painting in the world of art and wondered if that was an indication of where we were heading. He thought perhaps it was, but admitted he didn't really know. Nor did he especially feel we could anticipate a devastating experience for mankind—the nuclear disaster that would send us back to the era of the caveman. He was not prophesying the future; he was only analyzing the past and the present.

It is probably not insignificant that in later years Ernest made no reference to his theory of periodicity. It was clearly a tangent to his main preoccupation and Edith told me that he abandoned the theory altogether. My feeling was that he believed it had been worthwhile to put his observation into a systematic formulation, but he didn't want to devote any more effort to develop it further.

I couldn't get over how fertile his mind was, always moving in new directions and making new observations. He seemed to have an uncanny ability to see things that were not visible to others. For instance, he pointed out to me that there was a striking difference between the traditional architecture of the buildings in Europe and those in America. In Europe, the tops of the buildings seemed to be finished; there was a sense that they couldn't be extended beyond their present height. In America, one had the feeling that the tops of the buildings were "open," and that they could continue to rise higher and higher. He didn't mean that buildings literally were being added on to in America, but that there was a stylistic element in the architecture which reflected a basic cultural outlook. I thought this, too, was a very perceptive observation.

During all this period I was painting madly, two

or three canvases a week. Our small apartment at home was filling up with paintings which were propped against the walls and becoming something of a burden for the rest of the family. My mother, I think, was inwardly pleased that the new major influence on my life had been her personal discovery, and she was as quick to understand and respond to Ernest's theory as I was. My brother was less impressed. One day he said to me angrily that he thought my latest paintings were terrible. He was sure that I had misinterpreted Ernest's ideas and gone off in the wrong direction. I found it impossible to explain Ernest's ideas to him and simply shrugged off his criticism. My father also seemed to have difficulty in understanding what I found so engrossing in Ernest's theory, but he knew how seriously I was devoting myself to my painting and that was fine with him.

As time went on, it became increasingly clear to me that painting would be a primary interest in my life. After two years of college, I realized that I was learning much more from Ernest than from my formal studies. He was opening my eyes and mind to entirely new areas of knowledge, while in school my studies seemed to be a mere extension of what I already knew. So I asked Ernest one day whether he thought it would be all right if I quit school and just studied with him. (There was, incidentally, never any talk of money; the thought never even occurred to me that I or my family should pay Ernest for the time he was spending with me, even though I knew he was desperately looking for a university position to support Edith and himself. Our relationship was too deep and meaningful for that.)

Ernest said he would like to think about my question, and I respected him for his caution. I waited several days and then weeks for him to bring the subject up again. When he didn't, I decided to do so myself, and I told him that I had definitely decided to leave school. He smiled and seemed relieved. He said that it was fine with him, but that he didn't feel it was up to him to make the decision for me. It was mine to make. At the same time he urged me to talk it over with my parents to make sure they would approve.

Jubilantly, I announced my decision that evening at home—to a thundering silence. My father was stunned. He thought that studying with Ernest was fine but that could not be a substitute for getting a college degree. I explained that I was learning much more from Ernest than from school, and I didn't see why I should waste my life going to classes that meant nothing to me. My father didn't want to argue. He would call my Uncle Louis (Louis Finkelstein, his brother, was a well-known theologian and the scholar in the family) and ask his advice. Perhaps I could see Uncle Louis and talk it over with him.

Uncle Louis was sympathetic to my father's concern; but he said he knew nothing about art and would arrange for me to see his friend, Meyer Schapiro, a professor of art at Columbia University. That was all right with me, and after Uncle Louis talked to Meyer Schapiro, I called for an appointment. Professor Schapiro said he would be pleased to see me, and suggested I bring along some paintings so he could see what my work was like.

A few days later, I went up to see the professor (who later became a very good friend, and whose great text on Moissac was published in 1985 by

George Braziller along with my photographs [*The Sculpture of Moissac*]). I brought with me several paintings which were on a high level of tension, as a demonstration of what I had accomplished under Ernest's tutelage. I told Professor Schapiro about my experiences with Ernest and how much I was learning from him. To my delight, Professor Schapiro said he had heard of Ernest and knew something of his work. After looking at my paintings carefully, Professor Schapiro said, "You don't have to have a college degree to be an artist. I think your paintings are good. Zierer has helped you and you should by all means study with him." It was not the judgment I expected since I assumed Professor Schapiro would do his best to talk me into continuing at school. Now he was telling me just the reverse. I was exuberant. Triumphantly, I reported all this to my father, who not surprisingly was incredulous! But Uncle Louis said that if that's what Meyer Schapiro recommended, it was good enough for him.

And so when my school semester ended, a period of great and wonderful learning began for me. My schedule was simple: every morning I painted, and every afternoon I went to Ernest's apartment. We talked about my paintings and my writings. He and Edith read the short stories I wrote and they taught me how to work towards higher tension, how to recognize disintegrated breaks and correct them. It was a period in my life I shall never forget.

Soon I became aware that Ernest was doing more and more thinking about the psychological aspects of his theory: the mental processes by which integrated and disintegrated paintings were produced, and the significance of the levels of tension in terms of one's

49

individual personality. I felt I was studying with him at a time when a major new direction for his theory was emerging in his mind. He talked about Freud to me, and I began to read Freud so I could understand what Ernest was thinking. He also talked about the work of Gestalt psychologists, but while Freud's ideas were compelling to him, the Gestaltists were, from his point of view, moving in the wrong direction, at least as far as creativity was concerned. Thus, for instance, if you covered up a section of a painting that a Gestalt psychologist would consider integrated in his terms, its balance would be disturbed. It would no longer have that kind of unity the Gestaltists described. But if one covered up a section of a painting that Ernest called integrated, the rest would still be integrated. The difference was that the Gestaltists were referring to the design elements of a work of art and Ernest was talking about the bond between color elements. Gestaltists focused on what was in our minds as we looked at the painting. Ernest focused on what the artist had unconsciously put into the painting and was now the primary characteristic of its inner structure.

Ernest's concept of "an integrated whole" had no relationship to other aesthetic theories which used similar language to describe entirely different phenomena. At that time one of my great literary interests was James Joyce, and I talked to Ernest about *Dubliners*, *A Portrait of the Artist as a Young Man*, *Ulysses*, and *Finnegans Wake*. I told him that I was dazzled by Joyce's awareness of the smallest details in the human experience and his ability to weave these into a coherent whole. In "A Portrait," Stephen Dedalus defined "the rhythm of beauty" as "the first formal aesthetic relation of part to part in any aesthetic whole, or of an aesthetic whole to its part or parts, or of any part to the aesthetic whole of which it is a part." Stuart Gilbert elaborated on this theory in a footnote to his book on Joyce's *Ulysses* mentioning Coleridge's idea that "the sense of beauty subsists in simultaneous intuition of the relations of parts, each to each, and of all to a whole. . . ." Gilbert saw this as a paraphrase of Pythagoras' definition of Beauty as "the reduction of many to one."

Ernest's concept of an integrated whole seemed deeper than this aesthetic idea. His was emotional, unconscious, rooted in the essence of what constitutes the difference between living and non-living substances. Joyce's idea was intellectual, a construct of elements rather than a fusing of parts, a systematic organization of particles of experience rather than a living flow that incorporated the particles into a single being. A work of art classified by Ernest as disintegrated could be an aesthetic masterpiece from the point of view of Joyce's sense of unity. Indeed, I had a feeling that much of Joyce's writing was just that, and could be considered to be in the same class as Picasso's *Guernica*. I had a completely different feeling about Marcel Proust, Virginia Woolf, John Steinbeck and others who were favorite authors at the time and whose writings seemed to me to be consistently integrated. I still considered Joyce one of the all-time greats, but admired his works for different reasons.

In a sense, this distinction helped me understand why Ernest became increasingly attracted to psychology and decreasingly interested in aesthetics. He wanted to concentrate on the workings of the mind as it revealed itself in art rather than on the quality of works of art themselves. It was because of his study of depth psychology that Ernest first thought to change the terminology from organic and inorganic to integrated and disintegrated. I think he was searching for words that would be more meaningful in psychological terms; he also thought that in the translation from German to English, it would be an improvement. In addition, he felt that the term inorganic could be mistaken for Freud's disputed concept of Thanatos (the death instinct), which was not at all Ernest's meaning. Finally, using the verb to integrate would enable him to refer to the act of integrating, or the capacity to integrate, which was not possible with the word organic. I was a little sad to see the words organic and inorganic disappear from his lexicon, and wondered if he was making the right choice. Integration and disintegration were used in many other contexts and had meanings that had nothing to do with Ernest's categories. I was worried that people would misunderstand the precise characteristics to which he was referring in a painting. It would have been better, I thought, if he had coined new words to make it clear that he was referring to something different from other phenomena which had been previously described in psychology or aesthetics. Ernest agreed that his choice of words was a problem, but he liked integration and disintegration because they suggested psychological states which he felt were comparable to the qualities he was focusing on in paintings. He later modified the term integration by calling it color integration or element integration to denote a bond which exists between discrete particles in a work of art—color in a painting, space in a sculpture, words in a poem, etc.

The new terminology signaled his interest in applying his ideas to psychological therapy. At about that time, he began writing letters to psychiatric institutions to see if he could interest them in the idea of introducing a department of art therapy, or as he came to call it, "Creative Therapy," to distinguish his approach from other forms of art therapy which were beginning to become popular.

In the meantime, I had the idea of developing some courses on the Zierer theory so that others could learn about Ernest's ideas, and not incidentally, so he could begin to earn some money. The Master Institute of Arts on 103rd Street and Riverside Drive in Manhattan agreed to schedule such courses.

Once again my mother proved to be a source of strength, and with her help, we soon had several classes going—for both young and old. The income was hardly enough for Ernest to support himself, but it was a welcome supplement to what Edith was earning on her job. And I began to feel that I was launched on a career as Ernest's assistant and collaborator. The students in those classes included children of my mother's friends (no doubt some of those women who attended the Metropolitan Museum lecture series where she first met Ernest). They also included children I had become friends with at school or summer camp. (My sister, Helen, was one of those students, but for some reason my brother was not.) And my mother managed to interest a few adults who were either involved in the arts or were intrigued by the idea of trying their hand at painting.

It was in connection with those classes that Ernest first experimented with what initially he called "interference marks," but which at the students' suggestion, he came to call "push marks." These proved to be a major advance in the development of his theory and paved the way to its application in psychotherapy. He began by showing the students a selection of integrated and disintegrated paintings to teach them the difference. Then he told them to produce an integrated painting to get the feel of it. He explained that integrated paintings cannot be willed, or consciously produced; however, one can be "prepared" to let it "flow." The students would then paint an integrated painting, and if there was a disintegrated break, Ernest would point it out. At the next class the students would repeat the process. And then again a third time.

Finally, Ernest told the students about tension. But instead of going into detail about the three methods of raising the tension of their paintings, he said he would help them do so. After a student completed a fourth or fifth painting that was integrated and without breaks, Ernest would paint three small daubs of flat colors on top of the painting. These would be "push marks." He would ask the student to paint around the daubs to integrate them into the surrounding area—without painting over any part of the daubs. These daubs of color were a means of stimulating the student to paint at a higher level. Since the daubs were flat colors and painted with sharp edges, they were inevitably at a higher level of tension than the rest of the painting, and repainting the surrounding areas to produce integration would stimulate the student to achieve a higher level of tension in that part of his or her painting (Fig. M).

The imposition of the push marks was done with great care. Ernest would select the areas of the paint-

Fig. M: Push Marks on Completed Painting

ing which he thought would be most challenging to students when he painted his daubs of color. Moreover, choosing the color for each daub was a very deliberate process. Ernest's purpose seemed to be to find the place and the color which would pose the greatest stimulus to the student, creating high tension with adjacent colors and thereby forcing the student to apply himself or herself in order to produce an integrated painting. He also made sure that the push marks were disintegrated daubs in an integrated painting. I would never apply the push marks myself; that was the responsibility of the master. My job was to help students understand the difference between integrated and disintegrated paintings, and help them to recognize when they had succeeded in converting disintegrated areas into an integrated whole.

As time went on, Ernest invented a variation of the push marks. He would ask a student to make a drawing on a sheet of paper in preparation for a painting. Then he would impose the push marks on the sheet before the student began to paint—again very carefully choosing the area of a painting that would pose the greatest difficulty. This time his decision would not be based on the tension the push marks made with the adjacent colors, since there were no colors on the sheet; but he would try to put the daubs in a place that created a conflict with the subject drawn on the paper. Thus if the drawing were of a house in a landscape, Ernest might put one push mark in the middle of the house, another in the middle of the sky, and the third in the foliage of a tree. The student would then be asked to paint the picture —and integrate it completely. The goal seemed to be

Fig. N: First Push Mark Variation

to raise the student's consciousness about integration and tension while working on whatever the subject of the painting happened to be (Fig. N).

A third variation of push marks was to give a student a blank piece of paper and put three color daubs on the sheet before any drawing was made. This gave the student the freedom to create a drawing that might give some meaning to the push marks (a daub of color could, for instance, become a window; or by painting the surrounding area the same color as the push mark, its distinction could be eliminated). This was a different kind of challenge to the imagination of the student (Fig. O).

The next variation of push marks was as follows: Ernest would ask a student to do a drawing, and when it was completed, Ernest would draw a curve separating out one corner from the rest and then tell the student to paint the part of the picture contained in that corner. Then Ernest would paint push marks on the sheets, perhaps one in the painted area and the other two on the unpainted area. This was a way of combining the type of challenges posed in the first and second projects (Fig. P).

In between these special projects, Ernest would ask students to paint a picture of their choice without any interference. This was where my help was most valuable to students. Before meeting Ernest, I had studied painting and drawing at the Art Students League, and as Ernest's assistant I enjoyed the opportunity to display my skills as a more traditional teacher. I could help a student make a vase that looked like a vase, a tree that looked like a tree, a person that looked like a person. This gave the students a sense of satisfaction and achievement, and when

Fig. O: Second Push Mark Variation

they took their paintings home, they could show their friends that they had produced something that was recognizable as well as integrated.

Ernest couldn't have cared less about this aspect of our lessons, although he never voiced any objection to my playing this role. If someone was interested in learning to draw, that was fine with him. But as far as he was concerned, if a student covered a sheet with random color areas, that was as good as painting a recognizable subject. All Ernest wanted to do was to make a judgment about integration, disintegration, and tension. There were only two rules. The paintings had to be done with oil colors, since these were easier to control than watercolors or gouache. And there could be no blank areas left on the sheet; it had to be completely covered with paint. This wasn't because relatively small blank areas couldn't be integrated, but rather because large blank areas would simply be unpainted and therefore not subject to interpretation as either integrated or disintegrated. Also, he didn't suggest that watercolors were less likely to be integrated than oils, but that they might involve more random effects and not be as direct a function of the unconscious experience which produced integration. This ran counter to the common wisdom that one should only paint in oils after graduating from the "simpler" medium of watercolors, and it helped give students the feeling that they were starting at an advanced stage in the art of painting.

As time went on, Ernest kept inventing new ways of pushing the students. For instance, he would ask a student to paint a picture in fifteen minutes to show that neither integration nor tension were a direct function of time, but that some students did better

Fig. P: Third Push Mark Variation

61

under time pressure while others did less well. Another project was to paint a picture using only black and white colors (avoiding large areas of stark black and white which would be too hard integrate), to teach the students that they could achieve positive results even when forced to work within strict limitations. Still another was to paint a picture with one's favorite colors, and another with one's most disliked colors, again to expand the range of options in the creative process. A fourth project was to divide the paper into four sections, paint a single picture in what one thought was the highest possible level in one of the sections, and then repeat it in each of the other three sections, trying each time to raise the tension to a new height. This showed that even when students thought they had done their best, they could do still better when making a great effort.

There was one project with which I myself had difficulty; that was to produce a disintegrated painting. I was so fascinated with the almost magical way in which integration came out of one's brush that I couldn't quite see how to make disintegration come out. When Ernest suggested I try it, I painted in my usual way and tried to think of disintegration in the hope that it would work. It didn't and I was secretly proud of the strength of the integrative force within me. However, I did see some others accomplish the task with relative ease and wondered what the problem was. Ernest finally told me gently that my unconscious unwillingness to create a disintegrated painting might indicate that I had an excessive fear of death, and that I should try harder to produce the desired result since this could help me overcome my anxiety. (He later told me fear of disintegration may also be fear of inability to control destructive tendencies, directed either inwardly or outwardly.) This was the first time that I heard him relate one of his projects to a psychological phenomenon. I believed that his insight was correct and that he had discovered a secret about me which I had been unwilling to face. Once he had made the observation, I felt as if a switch had been turned on inside me. I approached the task of producing a disintegrated painting with a different point of view and this time had little difficulty in achieving the desired result.

Whether this had an effect on what Ernest described as my "excessive fear of death," I cannot definitely say. I do know that in my youth I used to wake up with a searing pain in my head caused by a dream that I was falling off a cliff and about to die. I assumed that it was one of those archetypal dreams which everybody experiences. But at some point they stopped, and it may well have been when I followed Ernest's advice and learned how to produce a disintegrated painting.

The Master Institute classes continued for several months with what appeared to be growing success. For a brief moment I felt that this might be the beginning of a Zierer School in the United States that would continue the work Ernest had begun in his Berlin School. But the Japanese had other plans, and on December 7, 1941 everything changed. America went to war and I had to come to grips with military duty. Soon after, I enlisted in a program to become an Air Force communications officer, providing that I could first complete my college course and obtain a degree. That ended the Master Institute courses, for although Ernest was the key to the program, without my (and my mother's) active support in organizing the whole project, he didn't feel he could continue. So he went back to his apartment on West 152nd Street to resume his search for an academic position, and I went back to City College.

There were significant changes in my resumed college career. In my first two years I had been at best a mediocre student, with a "C+" average. In my last 18 months, I became a straight "A" student, and I credited my work with Ernest as the cause of this change. Moreover, I had become accustomed to working for a living, so I got a job as night salesman at a New York bookstore, with hours from 5:30 p.m. to midnight, Monday through Saturday (earning the grand salary of $27 a week). My schoolwork flourished despite my working hours, but my painting time was severely curtailed. Also, correspondingly, I had little time to see Ernest.

II

It was shortly after I went back to college that Ernest was offered a position to join the staff of Hillside Hospital, a mental hospital (now called Long Island Jewish Medical Center, Glen Oaks, New York), to form what he decided to name a Department of Creative Therapy. (Besides his European Ph.D., New York State had certified him as a psychologist practicing psychotherapy.) His Creative Therapy Department was then the one and only art therapy department in the United States and probably in the world, independent of occupational, recreational and other "adjunct" therapies. Ernest wanted to emphasize the distinction from occupational therapy, which is why he proposed the term "Creative Therapy." (Today art therapies are at least as extensively utilized as conventional occupational therapy, but the art therapy that is practiced now bears little relation to Ernest's "Creative Therapy," which is based entirely on his theory.) The staff knew very little about art therapy in general, and nothing about Ernest's theory in particular (as there were as yet no English publications), but his credentials were impressive and his concept and approach to "painting therapy" seemed promising to the entire team. What made the appointment even more exciting was that shortly afterward Edith was appointed to head the Occupational Therapy Department of the hospital, and it was understood that eventually she would become Ernest's assistant.

In those early years of Ernest and Edith's work at Hillside, we saw each other only infrequently. I had a full program of courses at City College and a full-time job in the bookstore. I managed to continue to paint on weekends and Ernest's theory still dominated my thinking. But between his and my schedule, we had a hard time finding an hour or two to see each other. To make matters more complicated, the Zierers moved to Queens, which made commuting to Hillside much easier for them, but visiting them from Manhattan more difficult for me.

I was aware that Ernest was turning his attention increasingly to the psychological implications of his theory. He was fascinated by the relevance of integration and disintegration to the concept of psychic energy and felt that the insights found in psychoanalysis had a parallel in the phenomena he had discovered in the arts. He explained the process of integrating a painting as an activity which was identical to the process of solving a problem in life. (He had long used the verb "to solve" as a simplified form of saying "to produce an integrated painting." This was especially useful when there was a disintegrated break and he would explain to a student that the troublesome area should be solved by repainting it in order to make it integrated. Now the word solve helped to provide a bridge between the worlds of art and psychology.)

The "push marks" also took on a different meaning. Instead of considering them as stimuli for the artist, pushing him or her on to higher tensions, they became in Ernest's mind obstacles which needed to be solved. He was no longer dealing with budding artists who wanted to maximize their creative potential, but with patients who were striving to overcome their emotional and psychological difficulties. Since integration was a manifestation on a sheet of paper of the life force or psychic energy in a patient's mind, Ernest could exert a therapeutic influence by helping patients solve problems he imposed on them in his painting projects.

He began to see a correlation between his various projects and prototypical experiences in life, and he developed a sequence of projects which he felt presented a direct parallel to actual life situations. When he put his push marks on a blank piece of paper and asked the patient to paint an integrated painting without disturbing the marks, he felt he was testing the patient's ability to cope with life situations in which there were given obstacles to begin with, knowing at the outset that they were unchangeable.

When he put push marks on a detailed pencil sketch, he was presenting the patient with a situation in which careful plans had been made and unexpected obstacles arose. When the pencil sketch was completed and a corner marked off and painted before the push marks were imposed, it was like a life situation in which one was in the process of carrying out a plan when obstacles arose. When push marks were placed on a finished painting, the life situation was one in which plans had been fully carried out—when all of a sudden new obstacles arose.

With his students at the Master Institute, Ernest had hypothesized that the push marks would stimulate the artist to integrate on a higher level, and for the most part that's what happened. If it didn't work and the artist integrated on the same level he had been achieving in the past, or even on a lower level, Ernest simply tried another project, and kept experimenting until he found a project that did work. Indeed, he created new projects because he found that they had different effects on different students. Now the response of an individual patient seemed to be of primary significance. For if the patient was able to integrate at a higher level as a result of a particular push experiment, that could mean that he or she had a capacity to cope effectively with comparable conditions in his or her life. But if the patient integrated on a lower level, this was a clear sign that such conditions were difficult for the patient to deal with, and the patient would have to make a special effort to develop the capacity to cope more effectively with them in the future.

This train of thought produced an avalanche of new ideas. The speed project was a test of how well a patient did under time pressure. Painting with favorite colors indicated how well a patient did when things were going just as one wished. Painting with disliked colors showed how well a patient did when things were not going as one wished. The black and white project showed how a patient could cope with clearly defined limitations in life.

Once the basic concept had been developed, that painting was a way of acting out real life situations, many new projects could be invented. In fact there could be a project for every conceivable life situation, and the patient's response would provide an insight into his or her creative capacities to cope with that kind of problem.

The next task was to find a way to track the patient's response as more and more paintings were produced, and decide what could be done to help a patient cope with prototypical life situations which were giving trouble.

With this in mind, Ernest developed what he first called an "Integration Curve," and later changed to "Personality Profile," because it included both integrated and disintegrated paintings. A tension rating was given to each painting a patient produced and this rating was plotted on a chart. On the vertical scale of the chart, Ernest indicated the fourteen levels: A to A-7 and B to B-5, with B-5 the highest. (At times he used 21 levels, divided into C,D, and E. But his last version was in 14 levels.) On the horizontal scale, Ernest indicated the sequence of paintings, noting which project each painting represented. A painting could be either one of his special projects or just an "independence" painting. (These paintings could be in one of three categories, family, work or social independence, and they could be significant as a test of how a patient did when left to his or her own devices.) In the course of these paintings, Ernest would try to determine the highest level which each patient was reaching, or what Ernest called a person's "integrative capacity." This would enable Ernest to see when a patient performed below his or her capacity in certain life situations.

The fourteen levels indicated levels of tension. The lowest was virtually unheard of, and the highest was virtually unattainable. Most paintings would cluster around levels A-7, B, B-1 and B-2. To help make the judgment, Ernest selected a series of "standard" paintings to establish reference points for the rating process, and if one examined all standard paintings, it would be relatively easy to see that the tension was higher as one moved up the scale. The purpose of the standard paintings was not only to enable Ernest to make consistent judgments, but hopefully to be able to teach others to use his method in a systematic way.

As the paintings were produced, Ernest recorded the results in the patient's personality profile. He also kept the paintings themselves for future reference, having asked the patients to mark on the back of each painting the date and description of the project and to write a statement explaining the meaning of the painting. When disintegrated paintings occurred, which happened occasionally (particularly, as Ernest later discovered, with certain kinds of mental illnesses), he marked a point on the chart. Dotted lines indicated a project in which low integration is a plus. A full circle was used to indicate total disintegration. If three-quarters disintegrated, an almost full circle was shown. A half circle meant half the picture was disintegrated. A shallow crescent meant very small areas are disintegrated. A wiggling line, placed vertically, meant very small and scattered disintegration. This produced a profile of the creative performance of each patient, and each profile had its own distinct characteristics.

Armed with this data, Ernest now had the tools he needed to help patients improve their capacities to cope with life's problems. After a patient had done quite a few paintings, Ernest would repeat or assign related projects in which the patient had integrated on a comparatively low level to see whether he could help the patient do better in the same basic situation. He might also repeat projects in which the patient integrated on a high level. This was a way of testing the validity of the results. If roughly the same phenomena occurred on repeat projects, Ernest felt secure enough to make some judgments about the patient's psychological make-up. After a substantial number of additional paintings, a conference with the patient's psychiatrist was scheduled in which Ernest could explain what he had learned from the personality profile. He would point out those situations which had been mastered most successfully and those in which the patient had revealed some problems. Thus Ernest might deduce, from a relatively low level of integration in a painting with "favorite" colors, that the patient had difficulty dealing with success, or that the patient had masochistic tendencies and rejected experiences that were enjoyable, or that the patient had difficulty in deciding what he or she wanted. The descriptive notes patients had written, which sometimes were very extensive, reflected the patient's conscious evaluation of the problem situation, which could be compared to the unconscious response recorded in the integration/disintegration curve. These helped determine which explanation was relevant to an individual patient's life situation.

Ernest was gratified to discover that the patients reacted very positively to his judgments. They felt that somehow he had discovered a truth about their inner psyche of which they themselves had been unaware. He was always very sensitive to their feelings when he discussed their problem areas and encouraged them to believe that they could strengthen their capacities by repeating projects which had caused them to integrate or disintegrate on a low level. If, after a determined effort, they could achieve paintings on a higher level in troublesome projects, he was sure they would be able to deal with those situations more effectively in real life. This persuaded patients that Creative Therapy offered them an effective method to help them get better adjusted, and they would go back to their paintings with a renewed sense of purpose. Ernest discovered that under his therapeutic guidance, patients were able to improve their performance in the projects which had given them trouble. He also became aware that often a patient's progress or setback was apparent in painting projects before showing up in clinical settings. Treating psychiatrists and supervisors therefore came to look to Ernest as a remarkably insightful source of analytical information as well as therapeutic results.

It took five or six years of constant experimentation to work out this complex methodology. During that period, although I served for some time in the U.S. Air Force, I managed to keep up with the new directions Ernest's theory was taking. I saw some of the early standard paintings he selected and felt that I could come pretty close to determining the level of tension of a particular painting, although as in the case of disintegrated breaks, I considered Ernest's own judgment as the only infallible test.

I also became aware of publications that were beginning to appear about Ernest's work. I knew that he had written extensively in a variety of journals and books in the 1920s and 1930s as his early ideas crystallized. His first publication had appeared in Sweden in 1923, under the title "The Origin of the Baroque Cupola" (which was his Ph.D. thesis). This had been followed by several other publications written in German but published in Sweden, including "Laws of Art and Nature: New Ways of Research" (1924), and "Intuitive Paintings" (1927). Then there had been a series of German publications: "Classification of Art Values" (1930), "Reorganization of Art Criticism by Absolute Art Evaluation" (1930), and "Education in Art on the Basis of Absolute Art Evaluation" (1931). His last publication in Germany, foreshadowing his later interests, had been "Drawings by Children and Art Teaching." Then, in 1948, fifteen years later, he began publishing again, this time in psychological journals.

The first public statement about Ernest's work at Hillside was in a paper presented by I. Silberman, M.D. (the Hillside Hospital medical director who had originally hired Ernest) and published in the *Bulletin of the American Psychoanalytic Association* (September 1948), entitled "Art in Diagnosis." Following that there were several articles in the Jerusalem publication *Acta Medica Orientalia* (1950 and 1951) presenting a fairly detailed explanation of Ernest's original work in psychotherapy, and later articles in the *American Journal of Psychotherapy* (July, 1956) and elsewhere, describing some new directions in his theoretical development.

Ernest's use of the phrase "absolute art evaluation" had been important to him in his early years. As mentioned earlier, he had talked in terms of the absolute when I first met him, explaining that all other forms of art criticism were relative because they had to do with what was in the mind of the viewer, which could change from person to person, but since his approach had to do with what was in the painting and was unchanging, it was absolute. He felt there could be no difference of opinion about the values he was assigning to works of art.

When Ernest had described this concept, I had been convinced that he was justified in using the word "absolute." Subsequently, I came to feel that while such a terminology may have seemed appropriate to his European contemporaries in the 1920s, it was not in tune with the American intellectual climate of the 1940s. He must have come to the same conclusion, for by the time he started writing for psychological journals, it was definitely a thing of the past, except as a reference in his bibliography.

A detailed explanation of his theory written in English appeared in the second *Acta Medica Orientalia* article. I remember working with him to try—with limited success—to untangle his complicated Germanic sentences. I was skeptical that even then anyone reading the article would be able to understand what he was referring to, since his explanation was so abstract, but I was anxious to help him write whatever he could about his theory so that there would at least be something on record.

The article described the procedure of introducing his ideas to patients. The first step was what Ernest called a "Perceptual Experiment," and his writing shows how much difficulty he had with the language:

> The perceptual experiment lasts one and a half hours and consists in the presentation and, simultaneously, in the demonstration of twenty original paintings. This demonstration with paintings enables the patient, in an experimental way and through perception and recognition, to experience color-integration and color-disintegration as a pure emotional process, as an unconsciously determined interrelationship of the elements. It is emphasized that color- or element-integration is not based on the individual's intellectual or esthetic approach to the subject-matter but is, instead, the direct unconscious expression of the personality's emotional integration or ego-strength. Later the patient learns to understand, again emotionally, that element-integration can be carried through on a higher or lower level; in other words, the patient learns, through experience, that integration discloses ego-strength at different levels.

The twenty paintings were chosen to indicate various trends in art: subject matter, concepts of form, composition, color-harmony, etc. There were two selections for each trend, one integrated and one disintegrated. "By constant comparison," Ernest noted, "the patient is made to experience integration and disintegration and is helped only very little by circumscriptions like unity, color-connection, calmness, oneness, holding-together, or depth to denote integration, and color-disconnection, restlessness, chaos, or falling apart to characterize disintegration." The patients were urged to react to the paintings emotionally rather than logically. At the end of the session, Ernest wrote, patients are able to react to the paintings "spontaneously, directly and immediately," and recognize integration and disintegration without any difficulty.

At future sessions patients would be able "to mobilize their own potential capacities to integrate." They showed these capacities in their paintings, sometimes at their potential level and sometimes below it. This was a function of "the reality principle," which had to do with the process of maturation and the ability to transform the object-world into reality. "It takes some time," he wrote, for the maturing individual "to invest the object-world with feeling and significance," but the neurotic or psychotic person does not quite accomplish this goal. "Push tests" helped patients work towards fulfilling their potentialities. The push-colors were obstacle colors placed on a painting as a means of challenging the patients to higher achievement, higher coping ability, and helping them channel their aggression constructively by integrating the "obstacles" at higher color-tensions.

> In the frame of this short paper the statement must suffice that there actually is the possibility to distinguish between paintings with higher and lower levels of integration. Such levels are determined by what the writer calls "color-tension." There are rules which make it possible to raise and to lower the color-tensions consciously, though there are no rules whatsoever that would help to integrate them. In principle these rules show that color-ten-

sions are dependent upon the choice, the size and the location of colors. It is not necessary though or even advisable to explain these rules to the patient; certain arrangements in creative therapy (push-tests and projects) provoke, automatically, reactions towards an increase of color tensions. I repeat, increase of color-tensions is a conscious procedure and can, therefore, be accomplished by everybody, child and adult, normal and abnormal. Increase of tension *per se* is meaningless in creative therapy. Increase of tension is, however, highly meaningful in connection with the unconscious process of integration. When the patients are stimulated to raise their color-tensions gradually in the course of therapy, it is understood that they are to integrate their paintings at the same time. And this changes the situation decisively. Everybody is able to increase his color-tensions; but nobody is able to integrate the colors above his integrative capacities. There are limits for every individual and these limits are individually different. They are the integrative limits of our personality. The final aim of every psychological test is to determine, from one aspect or another, the strength or limit of the individual's capacities. Psychoanalysis takes the total personality into consideration. We too refer to the total personality when speaking of integrative limits.

During the course of treatment, patients were asked to disintegrate a painting in order to "become frankly and fully destructive," through a healthful disintegration, e.g. to destroy a symbiotic relationship. Schizophrenics, Ernest stated, react differently from neurotics to this project; the former found it easy to comply while the latter have some difficulty doing so.

In conclusion, Ernest referred to the personality profile as a means of schematizing for therapeutic and diagnostic purposes "the re-establishment or redevelopment of ego strength." He also mentioned three other tests which were in the process of being part of the Creative Therapy—the "Body-Space Test," the "Bipolarity Test," and the "Personality Structure Test" (stating that these tests were developed together with Mrs. Zierer)—but did not explain in this paper what they were. At around this time Edith was appointed associate director of the Creative Therapy Department and they became co-workers, sharing all duties, including the supervision of patients.

It was clear to me that in the few years since I had studied with Ernest his basic orientation had changed. The theory was the same and I was as enthusiastic as ever about it, but he was no longer concerned with how high a level of integration could be attained with his help. Trips to the Metropolitan Museum and the like had become a thing of the past.

I knew virtually nothing about psychology and psychoanalysis and so could make no judgment about the methodology Ernest had developed in Creative Therapy. However, I knew about integration, disintegration, tension, and push-projects and it all seemed quite logical to me. Moreover, I had over the years developed a belief in Ernest's near infallibility; he was such a remarkably intuitive person (intuitive in the traditional sense) that I found all of his ideas convincing. I worried to some extent about my uncritical acceptance of the new orientation of his theory and tried to be as objective and honest with myself as I could. But although I weighed carefully everything new I learned from him, I continued to believe he had a unique ability to look at paintings in a way that nobody else could, and I consider his discoveries a major breakthrough in the understanding of art.

As a matter of curiosity I visited Hillside Hospital several times to see how the patients reacted to Ernest and his ideas. At first I was a little apprehensive, since I had never been to a mental hospital before, but I soon discovered that the patients seemed quite "normal" and were enjoying their painting experiences in the same way that the Master Institute students did. It was clear that they all understood what Ernest was talking about in regard to integration, disintegration and tension, and they were having a good time testing out their abilities in the projects Ernest gave them. I was impressed just from an artistic point of view with the quality of the work being done and thought it was quite remarkable that a random group of people could produce paintings which under any other circumstances would be deemed noteworthy. Ernest smiled when I made this observation as if to say that he knew my head was still in the world of art, which was fine with him, but that now he was concerned with something quite different. It was as if there were two branches of the same tree, one art and one psychology, with the main trunk being the Zierer theory.

Ernest described his method as having application not only to therapy but to diagnosis as well. The patient's response to a particular project was one form of diagnosis, but he found a number of other approaches which were also significant. He was particularly interested in the differentiation between psychotic and neurotic patients, and he discovered two phenomena in his personality profiles which he believed were significant. The first was that psychotics did not, for the most part, integrate above level B. Try as they might, with one project after another, they rarely went beyond this limit. The second phenomenon was that schizophrenics showed what Ernest called "scatter" in their personality graphs. This meant that periodically, for no apparent reason, they would produce a disintegrated painting. Their responses were unpredictable, and their disintegration inexplicable. This would be reflected in a scattered curve, with points appearing periodically in a graph of at least fifteen to twenty projects.

The low level of the personality profile, Ernest believed, not only signified the repression of a psychotic's integrative capacity, as was the case with neurotic patients, but an actual and definite limitation of his or her potentialities. In his *Acta Medica Orientalia* article, he described this as "withdrawal of integrative capacity or . . . withdrawal of libido or psychic energy from the object-world." As for scatter, he believed that this was a function of the psychotic's ability to disintegrate on the same level as he integrated. When a neurotic patient was told to disintegrate, he would tend to increase color tensions beyond his limits to achieve the desired result; but the psychotic patient was equally at home with the destructive drives evident in disintegration as with constructive drives represented by integration. He moved from one to the other with ease and often for no apparent reason.

Curiously, "the body-space test," which was the subject of Ernest's first *Acta Medica Orientalia* article published in 1950, had nothing to do with integration, although it was another demonstration of Ernest's remarkable discoveries about the human personality through his unique way of observing paintings. He described it as a component of Creative Therapy, which is "an entirely new approach developed by this writer."

Ernest explained that the body-space test was administered to every patient admitted to Hillside Hospital. It was a differential test between neurosis and psychosis and consisted of five drawings in crayon. By the time the article was written, the test had been administered to 1,800 patients, and according to Ernest, had demonstrated about an 86 percent reliability when compared with the clinical discharge diagnoses. (In 1951 and 1955, a further validation study was made on the test which was described in a second article.)

To explain the theoretical basis for the test, Ernest began with a perceptive observation about primitivity:

> Primitivity in drawings is always associated with poverty of content and form. In this sense the term primitivity is often identified with pathological regression. Many healthy people, however, draw in a primitive way when not taught how to draw realistically. Many normal artists paint in a primitive style for some artistic reason—i.e., they use poor content and form intentionally. Far regressed psychotics with artistic training often draw in a highly realistic style. Primitivity in art as opposed to realism is not too reliable as a diagnostic determinant. Neither identification of primitivity with regression nor identification of realism with progression are considered in creative therapy. Both the concept of

primitivity and the concept of realism are based on content and form. Content and form, however, are disregarded in creative therapy altogether. And yet, the superficial association of regression with primitivity of content and form is no reason to give up the term regression for diagnostic purposes. The body-space test is, in fact, based on the problem of regression but regression is here purely an evolutionary phenomenon.

The nature of regression, as Ernest used the term, was reflected in five drawings the patient was asked to make. The first was to consist of a simple landscape showing the ground, the sky and a tree. The second was to represent a steep hill and a house and trees on the slope of the hill. The third was a view out the window with perhaps a building, the lawn, a tree and the sky. The fourth was a copy of any landscape painting. And the fifth was any subject from imagination.

Ernest found evidence of regression in the primitivity of a patient's understanding of space through an analysis of these crayon drawings. Psychotic patients showed stages of regression which he called "horizontal stratification, transparency, horizontal ratification, ramification, peripherally oriented panorama, centrally oriented panorama."

"Horizontal stratification" was a stage of regression in which body and space were separated, as was evident when the sky was drawn in a blue ribbon on top and the ground in a green ribbon on the bottom and the patient insisted that this depicted reality. Empty space was a concrete object. When shown in the second drawing project "looking out the window," that the world did not look as if it were separated by "emptiness," psychotic patients would tend to say that "it may not look that way but that's the way it is." This revealed a world view which could be found among young children in the latency period of development, and Ernest considered horizontal stratification as evidence of regression to the anal stage. This could be confirmed if in the second painting the house and tree were drawn vertically from the slope of the hill rather than vertically on the paper—this was called "ramification," which was an indication of a regressed body-space orientation.

Further regression, to the oral stage of development, among psychotic patients was revealed by a "centrally or peripherally oriented panorama," where objects such as a house and a tree were arranged around the center or the periphery of the paper, rather than oriented to the horizontal base of the paper. "Here the individual is not interested in the outside world," Ernest wrote. "He is interested in his own position. First, as a narcissistic observer standing outside (in the centrally oriented panorama), secondly as an omnipotent ruler being the center of things (in the peripherally oriented panorama)."

Neurotic patients would show a three-dimensional sense of space, with things existing behind or above other things. Hence the body-space test was an effective diagnostic tool which could distinguish between stages of regression.

The same year that this first article appeared, Ernest introduced his concept of "Bipolarity in Diagnosis Through Art" in an article in the *American Journal of Psychotherapy*. Here, too, he ventured into territory beyond his basic concept of integration and disintegration and reported several new observations about the inner dynamics of a painting and their relationship to specific mental states. He was concerned about bipolarity as a "function of opposite forces."

I remember that when he was preparing this paper, I had become conscious of certain contradictory statements in philosophy and literature. Ernest was eager to know about them because of his developing ideas on the significance of bipolarity. (I recalled my discussions with him when, years later, I encountered William Blake's "contraries" in *The Marriage of Heaven and Hell*, and came across the lines of T.S. Eliot's *Four Quartets*: "in my beginning is my end . . . what you are is what you are not . . . what you do not know is the only thing you know . . . the way up is the way down. . . .") Ernest speculated that bipolarities could be resolved by normal people who would find a way to make them compatible with each other, and by neurotics who would find ways to make compromises. However, among psychotics bipolarities appeared to be incompatible. He identified several categories of bipolarities to illustrate his observations.

One experiment he described in connection with what he called "evolutionary bipolarity" was especially intriguing. It involved forty patients—some neurotic and some psychotic—who were asked to paint a portrait in oil from a plaster model. They were told to express as close a resemblance to the model as possible. "The result," Ernest wrote, "was remarkable. The paintings showed little resemblance to the model, but all paintings showed some resemblance to the patients who painted them." Ernest stated that those which were painted by schizophrenics showed the greatest resemblance to themselves. He added that "one could say that all these portraits were self-portraits, although of course they were not intended to be that. The patients portrayed themselves unconsciously, though consciously they tried to make a portrait of the model." (The proponents of the recent theory that the *Mona Lisa* was a self-portrait of Leonardo da Vinci would do well to study Ernest's observations that all portraits tend to be self-portraits to some degree.)

The evidence of bipolarity in self-portraits was explained by Ernest as a conflict between one's narcissistic tendencies and the "social interest" involved in representing another person. Among schizophrenics, this represented an "incompatible opposition." They knew their own body better than anything else and therefore produced a striking self-resemblance. Normal and neurotic individuals, however, tended to resolve the problem by developing their "individual style" in their portraits while achieving some resemblance to the model being portrayed.

Another form of bipolarity had to do with integration and disintegration, which Ernest briefly described in his article. Schizophrenics alternated between the two at random, while neurotics and so-called "normal" people disintegrated only when they raised the intensity levels of their paintings beyond their ability to cope with stress. Two other somewhat esoteric forms of bipolarity were mentioned—one called "contiguous bipolarity" which had to do with the different ways in which schizophrenics and neurotics handled conflicting forces represented in the subject matter of a particular painting, and a second called "interpretive bipolarity" which referred to the psychotic's tendency to substitute symbolism for reality. In conclusion, Ernest repeated his belief that "compromise" was typical of neurosis, "compatibility" was typical of "normality," and "the incompatibility of opposites" was characteristic of schizophrenia. He also stated that creative therapy had developed methods for transforming "conflicts" found in abnormal art into "problems" that could be solved, with the caveat that the incompatible bipolarities of schizophrenia were not transformable. Psychotics had no concept of "symbolism." To them symbols were concrete reality, as real as hallucinations.

I continued to be fascinated by Ernest's thought processes and was able to follow, for the most part, the twists and turns of his theoretical development. But my personal interest continued to be my own painting. Ernest saw my work from time to time and would occasionally make a comment about a painting that was particularly strong (on a high level of integration), or call my attention to a break I had overlooked. But he was not involved particularly in my development as an artist. Even later, when I had two one-man exhibitions, one at the New School and one at a Madison Avenue gallery, Ernest came to the openings as a teacher who was proud of the progress of his student, but not as one who was involved in the contemporary art scene.

As part of my professional life I became active in the museum world. Because of these growing involvements I talked to Ernest about the possibility of an exhibition which would introduce the Zierer theory to the art world. He thought this would be a fine idea and we spent some time thinking of how we might use the work of Hillside Hospital patients for such a project. This was at a time when Dubuffet and artists of the Art Brut school were coming into prominence and there was some interest in paintings by the mentally ill. Unfortunately, when I broached the notion of a Zierer exhibition to curator friends of mine, it was only the aspect of paintings by the mentally ill which aroused their interest, not the Zierer discovery of integration, disintegration and tension; and I was never able to arrange the kind of exhibition I had in mind.

Occasionally Ernest and I would have a conversation about art as distinguished from art therapy. My wife and I were beginning to acquire works of art for our home—by Moore, Giacometti, Arp, Marini, Manzù, Calder and others; and we had become personal friends of several of these artists. But this was a world with which Ernest had lost contact. We had the strange feeling that although the knowledge we had gained from Ernest was the foundation of our experience of and response to works of art, he was strangely uninvolved in our development as collectors or participants. To the extent that he thought about art at all, his mind was on the twenties and thirties—or even earlier—when that had been his primary interest. He mentioned, for instance, that when Braque and Picasso were painting works that were almost indistinguishable from each other, Braque's paintings tended to be on a higher level of integration. He also said that Matisse's work was more consistently integrated than Picasso's. These and other remarks of his about artists whose works he knew well were always in my mind as I visited galleries and museums, and invariably I found evidence to support his observations. We talked about copies of paintings and forgeries which appeared in the news from time to time, and he pointed out that a copy could actually be "better" than an original since it could be integrated on a higher level. I felt that he had a much deeper sense of the meaning of originality than was generally accepted. The unique individuality was manifested in the brushstrokes and nuances of a painting, even when it was a literal copy of another painting. He saw nothing less original in copying a painting than in copying nature or even painting abstract forms. He acknowledged that "the original" painting was more important from an art historical point of view, but in a deeper sense the "copy" was as much of an original as the "original." The same was true of translations. The famous statement that "poetry is that quality which is missing in a translation" could mean in Ernest's terms that the original was integrated and the translation disintegrated, or that the translation was at a lower level of integration than the original. This would happen because the aura around words in one language, created by all the nuances surrounding those words, was different from the nuances of the equivalent words in another language. Thus the inner quality created in the original could not be directly recreated in a translation into another language. Integration and tension were functions of those auras and defined the inner quality of the creative work. As I thought about that phenomenon, I realized that English translations of some contemporary poets are consistently integrated in translation, as with the Greek poet Cavafy, or the French poet St.-John Perse, while classical poets like Virgil and Dante are far more difficult to integrate in translation

The whole question as to what integration is and how it came about in a work of art continued to puzzle me. When I first met Ernest, he had described it as part of the same process which created integrated life. A biological organism was indisputably alive; a disintegrated object was not alive. But what was responsible for life was unknown. I had asked Ernest whether he thought that at some future time man would be able to create life in the laboratory, and his answer was an unqualified "No!" I wondered how he could be so sure. It was as mystifying to me as Einstein's statement that nothing in the universe could move faster than the speed of light. But Ernest was adamant. Now that psychology had become his preoccupation, he liked to refer to psychic energy and integrative capacities rather than organism, but this didn't help me grasp the nature of the phenomenon. Despite the seeming impossibility of finding an answer, I never doubted—and never have doubted in the almost fifty years I have known about it—the certain reality that integration and disintegration exist in works of art and that their existence is of profound significance.

In the 1950s my wife and I periodically spent social evenings at the Zierers where we met quite a few of the psychiatrists who were on the staff of Hillside Hospital. I could see that Ernest was held in high esteem by them, and I thought this might be because of his gentleness, his obvious intelligence, and their recognition that he was an original thinker who was foraging in unknown territory. I imagined that these psychiatrists or psychoanalysts felt at home with the idea of an integrated personality, but wondered if they were able to see integration in a painting. My hunch was that because these were terms which had relevance in their own work, they assumed Ernest was referring to the qualities with which they were familiar in another context. There were several psychiatrists who seemed to have a sensitive understanding of Ernest's ideas, including his good friend Dr. Hans Kleinschmidt (who was a co-author with Ernest in an *Acta Medica Orientalia* article), but I wondered if any of them could tell whether a painting was integrated or disintegrated, or whether he just understood the principles on which Ernest's theories were based.

Although Ernest was in his own quiet way the magnet which drew his colleagues together, it was Edith who was usually the center of attention at those evening gatherings. She was the hostess, the outgoing personality who made everybody feel at home, always laughing and full of good cheer. She obviously loved her career, first as the head of the Department of Occupational Therapy, and then as Associate Director of the Department of Creative Therapy, and finally as Director of the Department after Ernest's retirement in 1960. And she also played the role of translator of Ernest's ideas and sentiments since her command of English was better than his. He continued to be somewhat shy and reserved even when he was with friends, while Edith was more social and articulate.

Ernest told me, and I heard confirmation of this during exchanges at those social evenings, that he was playing an important role in the weekly conferences held by the Hillside Hospital staff to discuss specific patients. At these conferences the psychiatrist in charge of the case would present a report on the condition of the patient, giving a diagnosis of the illness and describing the progress (or lack of it) made

during the period of hospitalization. Every department was represented at the conferences, and this
would include Ernest who would explain what he
had learned through his various projects and present
his interpretation of the results recorded in the personality profile. Ernest and Edith's friends whom I
met at their social evenings confirmed Ernest's observation to me that there was often a remarkable corre-
spondence between his findings and those of the psychiatrists in charge of the cases. When Ernest noted
his findings based on the patients' paintings, the psychiatrists accepted them as they would lab tests performed by a specialist with a proven track record of
making accurate diagnoses. The observations Ernest
made about various aspects of the patient's illness,
based on an analysis of individual projects or the
results of his various tests, provided insights which
were felt to be uncannily revealing. And when
Ernest's analysis disagreed with clinical appraisals, as
for instance when a patient was thought to be psychotic but Ernest found that the level of integration of
some paintings had been on a consistently high level,
it turned out that Ernest's diagnosis was borne out by
subsequent findings. So he was earning the respect of
many of his colleagues, even though the basis for his
observations was a mystery to them.

True, there were some who couldn't understand
what Ernest was doing or even what he was talking
about when he referred to aspects of a painting that
neither psychiatrists nor artists had ever heard about.
They suspected that "Creative Analysis" might be little more than one of those crackpot theories that kept
cropping up on the fringes of psychoanalysis or art
criticism. But even these doubters were struck by the

remarkable accuracy of Ernest's perceptions at the weekly conferences.

As Ernest's ideas proved their validity in different ways I became convinced that one day they would explode publicly as one of the great discoveries of our time. Although I had recognized from the beginning how difficult it was to communicate accurately the key elements of his theory, his ultimate recognition seemed inevitable. I had a profound faith in the method by which history accorded towering figures their rightful place; and although I had come to know a number of individuals who were famous in their fields, no one loomed larger in my mind as a seminal figure than Ernest. I felt he had discovered something as fundamental as the DNA of art; when fully explained, it would have enormous implications for the way the creative process is understood. Art historians, art critics, museum curators and artists, to say nothing of psychiatrists, psychoanalysts, and psychologists, would all greet Ernest's theory as a major new insight into the nature of art and its relation to life.

Soon I found myself wondering whether I had a responsibility to take the lead in winning recognition for Ernest's ideas. In my working life I was in the public relations business and was supposed to know something about the manner in which important developments (and some not so important!) achieved visibility. Why shouldn't I do something about Ernest's discoveries?

My first step in this direction was to try to become a member of the board of trustees of Hillside Hospital. It was not easy to accomplish this since I did not have any of the attributes which would make someone a likely candidate for board membership of a mental hospital. Some members of the board were wealthy people who could make substantial financial contributions; others were leaders in the Jewish community (Hillside Hospital was one of a large number of medical institutions which was heavily supported by the Federation of Jewish Philanthropies). Still others had developed an attachment to Hillside Hospital because of personal experiences in their families, such as relatives who had suffered from a mental illness and had been helped by the hospital or a member of the hospital staff. And some had suffered from a mental disorder themselves and were eager to do their part to help others. I didn't qualify for any of these reasons.

However, I speculated that my role as chairman of what had become by then one of the major public relations firms in the country might well be of interest to the board. That could enable me to make a professional contribution to the hospital as a trustee. Dr. Joseph Miller, who was the director of the hospital at the time, sensed that I could be a valuable resource in connection with the hospital's own public relations needs. The chairman of the board, whom I met through Dr. Miller, agreed. And so did others on the board. My friendship with the Zierers was considered incidental to my desire to be of public relations help to the hospital as a whole. My interest was welcomed and in a relatively short time, I was invited to join the board.

In the next several years, I felt I was playing a secret role comparable to the Count of Monte Cristo. To all appearances, I was a prime mover on the board, but my secret purpose was to win recognition for Ernest's earthshaking discoveries.

Hillside Hospital had given him the opportunity

to apply his theories to mental illness, but now I wanted the Hospital to provide the platform on which his theories could win their deserved recognition. My goal was to bring Ernest's work out into the open and help it take its place as one of the monumental discoveries of our time.

Ernest himself was not involved in my plan and never gave any evidence of seeking the kind of recognition I wanted for him and his work. He looked at my involvement on the board of Hillside Hospital as no more than an opportunity for us to continue to work together. The theoretical development of his ideas was all that counted for him. His and Edith's articles were appearing with regularity—an average of one a year during the 1950s and 1960s. (Today the bibliography of articles by the Zierers and others on Creative Therapy includes over 50 publications.) The number and variety of painting projects continued to grow—with some patients having as many as 250 paintings recorded in their personality profiles. Patient hospitalization periods could be as long as a year, and if they participated in Creative Analysis, the schedule included two hours a day, four times a week. A vast collection of paintings by patients came into existence—over twenty thousand—each carefully rated according to Ernest's categories and noted on patients' personality profiles. I was astounded at the size and scope of this treasure trove and knew that it contained an invaluable resource for the study of Ernest's theory. But Ernest was incapable of thinking in grandiose terms about what he had accomplished. His only desire was to keep working, and the new discoveries he was making were reward enough for his labor. If I talked to him about my personal goal to make sure that his discoveries would not be lost to future generations, his face would assume his characteristic pained expression, as if he wanted to say, "David, I know how keenly you feel about this, and you should by all means do what you feel you must. But for myself, I haven't the slightest desire to win fame or glory. And if it should turn out that my work disappears after my lifetime, it would be sad, but I recognize that we must accept the whims of history."

It was ironic that in my professional life as a public relations practitioner, I lived in a world which placed a high value on recognition, while one of the greatest men I knew personally didn't care in the least about achieving it. Ernest was without doubt the most humble man I ever met. And quite understandably, Ernest's humility drove Edith to distraction. As a practical and devoted wife, she felt that Ernest was paying a price for his reserve. He could have far more resources for his work if he were more aggressive about promoting his accomplishments. She believed in what I was trying to do and we became partners in trying to call attention to Ernest's work despite his lack of interest.

The task was formidable. My role-playing on the board was more challenging than I thought it would be. Dr. Miller never showed any special interest in Ernest's work and my fellow trustees hardly knew he existed. My hopes picked up somewhat when Dr. Miller was replaced by Dr. Lou Robbins who came to Hillside Hospital from the Menninger Clinic and who seemed more open to new ideas. In time, I decided to let him in on my private plans, and after one of our board meetings, I told him about my desire to help make Ernest's obscure theories accessible to the world. To my delight, Dr. Robbins was sympathetic. "I have no doubt that you are right," he told me, "and that probably no one at the Hospital knows what Ernest is doing. I certainly don't," he said. "The problem is that Dr. Zierer's articles are totally incomprehensible. They seem to be a mixture of psychoanalytical terms with observations about a new way of looking at paintings that none of us can understand. However," he added, "we know very little about the treatment of mental illness. The placebo rate of recovery for the kind of illnesses we find at Hillside is about 22%, and with all the techniques we presently employ, including psychotherapy, shock treatment, and medication, we can raise the recovery rate to about 27%. That's no great accomplishment. At the same time, we know that there are some people who have an intuitive ability to help patients. We don't know why, but we know that what they do works. Dr. Zierer is one of those people, and what he does helps patients. Whether it is because of his personality, his sensitivity, his caring, or whether he has developed a method that could be practiced by others, we cannot tell. He certainly has difficulty letting others in on his secret, and if you believe you can help, you ought to do so."

That was good news! Now it was up to me to figure out what the next step should be. I knew that the prospect of teaching others how to practice creative therapy and validating its effectiveness were the two overriding goals. Why not develop a major research project to validate Zierer's theory and see whether it could be replicated by other therapists in other institutions? If the research results were positive, Creative Therapy Departments could be set up in other hospitals and become a major contribution by Hillside Hospital to the field of psychotherapy.

After discussing the idea with Ernest and Edith, I proposed this project to the board. The question was raised as to why so much effort should be put into Creative Therapy, a relatively minor function at the Hospital. Why not validation projects for other types of treatment? I tried to answer without revealing my personal feelings about Ernest, but had difficulty dealing with some of the more aggressive questions. Finally, Dr. Robbins came to my rescue by suggesting that my idea be taken up with the Medical Board of the Hospital. The consensus was that if the Medical Board approved the idea, and if the necessary funds did not come out of the operational budget for the Hospital but were raised from independent sources, the project would be acceptable.

However, my meeting with the Medical Board led to other obstacles. Although I could impress some of my fellow lay-board members with my knowledge of Creative Therapy, the physicians on the Medical Board were totally unresponsive. As far as they were concerned, Creative Therapy was simply another name for Occupational Therapy. The idea of "validating" Zierer's theory made no sense at all to them. I tried to explain that Zierer's method was based on his unique observations about the relationship between color particles in a painting. I said that I had studied with Zierer some years ago and was familiar with his method. But if others were ever going to be able to apply his techniques, some objective method of determining the quality of those relationships in patients' paintings would have to be developed. Perhaps new electronic scanning devices being developed at the time could feed impulses into a computer, and a way could be found to "read" a painting electronically. Zierer's subjective evaluation would then be replaced by a standardized method and hence form a more reliable means of making judgments.

My presentation was totally unconvincing. Although I knew that some members of the Medical Board had shown a genuine interest in Ernest's work in the past, one of the current members seemed to be speaking for his colleagues when he said condescendingly, "I know that when somebody has been helped by therapy, it is natural to be grateful to the therapist. Clearly you have good reason to be thankful to Dr. Zierer and we can understand your enthusiasm." I protested that I had never been Dr. Zierer's patient, but this only produced sympathetic smiles. Dr. Robbins suggested that no harm would be done if I explored the possibility of securing funds for the kind of project I had in mind. "Fine," they said, "but not as a Hillside Hospital project." They wished me luck!

What was I to do? Could an application be made to foundations for a grant without official Hospital sanction? How much money would be needed? What facilities would be used to conduct the research? I made some rough guesses and wrote a request for funds on my company stationery to a half-dozen foundations which supported medical research, asking whether they might be interested in considering a proposal on a validation project. The answers were all a polite "No."

My efforts to help Ernest continued in various forms during my years on the board, but they never proved successful. I earned the gratitude of the institution by providing the public relations help I had promised, but this never proved to be of help to Ernest. Eventually I resigned in frustration.

My unhappy experiences with the medical community about Ernest's ideas did not in any way lessen my conviction about the validity of his discovery or my belief that somehow an objective way could be found to record what I knew was a fundamental reality about art. Every now and then I would come up with a new idea. For instance, once, when Ernest was hospitalized for six weeks with a coronary, I talked to him about making a film showing how he explained the difference between integration and disintegration. At another time I worked with a research engineer to see whether an electronic scanning system could be developed to detect Ernest's categories. Ernest was always willing to cooperate and said he would do anything he could to help. But his heart was never in it, and there were other things in my life which demanded my attention. So we never got beyond the talking stage.

During this time, Ernest was very attentive to my family, particularly my mother. In the latter years of her life she became subject to periodic depressions, and Ernest recommended a psychiatrist, Dr. Ernest Altman, who was very helpful in her times of need. But the depressions persisted. I suggested that she work with Ernest for a while, thinking perhaps more in terms of "painting lessons" than treatment. Ernest was very fond of my parents, and he and Edith considered them their American family. He was delighted with my idea of "teaching" my mother how to paint. He knew that it had been her "discovery" of him at the Metropolitan Museum which had brought us together and that she had always been pleased by our relationship. He was her "find." Ernest was eager to be of help and devised a special painting program for her.

My mother had always taken great pride in my paintings, and in the last year of her life she enjoyed sitting for a double portrait I did of her and my father. But her own paintings turned out to be a surprise, even to her. They were remarkably strong and integrated on a high level, and she was pleased with her accomplishments. Some of her paintings had special symbolic meanings, as with a painting of a tree with several trunks and branches which represented her relationship to each of her three children and her husband. If she had lived longer, I think she might have become a serious painter. My father also "studied" with Ernest. But he didn't take it as seriously as my mother did. He didn't have the same emotional kinship with Ernest, and his painting became more of an intellectual exercise than a deeply felt experience.

Ernest was forced to retire from Hillside Hospital in 1960 at the age of 68. Edith took his place as Director, but Ernest for the first time since I had met him seemed to lose his drive. My wife and I continued to visit Ernest and Edith in their Queens apartment and found that a whole evening could go by with Edith playing cheerful hostess to three or four couples with Ernest hardly saying a word.

Edith also became more aggressive in their work and took an increasing position of leadership in developing new projects, organizing lectures and preparing articles. She had received the official recognition of "Registered Art Therapist" status and had become a gifted therapist herself. She began to feel that it was up to her to carry on for both of them and eventually became an author in her own name of articles on Creative Therapy, continuing on after Ernest's death. One of the most interesting of her earlier articles appeared in 1966 on "The Role of Creative Analysis in Family Treatment," as a two-part article in the *Bulletin of Art Therapy*. This described a development in which she had played a major role, namely working with various members of a family on a joint painting, with each member having the responsibility to integrate his or her section with contiguous sections painted by other members of the family. This seemed to open up an entirely new direction for the application of Creative Therapy techniques.

Although my wife and I were very much removed from the psychological development of the Zierer theory, we continued to think of Ernest's contribution to our understanding of the arts every time we visited a museum. Over the years we would often be in a gallery and suddenly exclaim, "That painting is intuitive!" Since we were traveling a good deal, I began to make notes about intuitive works of art that we came across (as I still do to this day), reliving as it were Ernest's initial experience of cataloging such works. We were convinced that two works of architecture we had seen were intuitive—the Palazzo Vecchio in Florence, Italy, and the Taj Mahal in Agra, India. The buildings seemed to float in the air in front of our eyes, and they made us dizzy to look at. We consider Florence almost our second home, visiting it two or three times a year for over twenty years; and I have never changed my mind about the glorious quality of the Palazzo Vecchio. I also am certain that Bronzino's *Venus and Cupid* in the National Gallery in London is intuitive (although it is in a gallery which includes masterpieces by Michelangelo, da Vinci, Raphael, Correggio, the Bronzino glows as if it had a light inside it which none of the other paintings possesses). Some of the other paintings which I believe are intuitive are the Grünewald *Isenheim Altarpiece* in Colmar, France; the central panel of Rogier van der Weyden's *Last Judgment* in Beaune, France; the Hieronymus Bosch *Garden of Delights* in the Prado; the ceiling fresco by Pietro da Cortona in the Barberini Palace in Rome; the Pinturicchio paintings in the Library of the Duomo in Siena; the Giovanni Bellini *St. Francis* in the Frick Collection; Pelizza da Volpede's *Il Quarto Stato* in the Museum of Modern Art in Milan; the Piero della Francesca portraits of the *Duke and Duchess of Umbria* in the Uffizi; and Peter Brueghel's *Winter* in the Kunsthistorisches Museum in Vienna. I believe Michelangelo's *David*, Michelangelo's *Madonna* in the Medici Chapel, and Donatello's *Magdalen* in the Museo dell' Opera del Duomo in Florence, have that same glowing, floating, ethereal quality. There is a mosaic, also in the Museo dell' Opera del Duomo in Florence, which I believe is intuitive: *San Zenobi* by Monti di Giovanni. And I have notes about dozens of other works of art I have come across—some by well known artists, others by artists I never heard of—which I think are also intuitive.

I never mentioned any of this to Ernest, since after twenty years of work at Hillside Hospital he seemed to feel that his origins in the world of art had been merely a prelude to his work in psychology. Even when he gave a series of courses at the New School in the early 1960s, he made little if any reference to the great art of the past; art for him had become the means to help people cope with life's problems. I understood and respected his feelings but worried that what to me had been a monumental discovery in the field of art might be lost. The application of the Zierer method in psychotherapy was surely significant, but I felt that in a curious way its psychological ramifications added further proof of its significance in the creative world of art.

More serious was the question of what would happen to all of his ideas now that Ernest had retired. As he became less and less communicative, I felt he had resigned himself to the decline of his energies and even his faculties. He had become hard of hearing, which compounded his problem with the language; his heart was giving him trouble and he had developed a rare form of life-threatening cancer.

For five or six years after Ernest retired, the Zierers continued to live in their Queens apartment. In 1964 they bought a small house in Danbury, Connecticut, on Candlewood Lake, and when they moved into their new house, Edith set up one of the rooms as an archive for the materials they had accumulated at Hillside Hospital. Tragically there was a flood at the Hospital in 1976. As a result, they were not able to save a large number of paintings by patients as well as clinical and Creative Therapy records. There was still enough to tell the whole story if some means could be found to present Ernest's theory to the world, but with Ernest withdrawing more and more into himself, the prospect of this happening while he was alive seemed increasingly remote.

Ernest and Edith were invited to visit Germany in 1962 and they were treated as celebrities, with interviews in the press and receptions organized by former students. In 1965 they were invited again, this

Ernest and Edith Zierer
Danbury, Connecticut, June, 1965

time to lecture in various universities and participate in a major colloquium. Edith did most of the work to prepare the lectures and gather materials for exhibitions of patients' paintings. Their night flight to Germany in September, 1965 was uneventful, both of them catnapping on the way. Edith woke up shortly before arrival, but Ernest did not. He died in his sleep. He was 73 years old.

Incredibly, Edith managed to survive the ordeal, make arrangements for Ernest to be cremated, and arrive at the Colloquium in time to deliver the papers that she and Ernest were to have given together. Her presentation was so impressive that she was asked to stay on an extra three days to participate in follow-up discussions. After that she was able to continue on to the other universities to deliver the remaining lectures that had been planned. Her energy and determination were astounding to everybody who knew what had happened.

Several weeks after Ernest's body was cremated in Germany in September, 1965, the ashes arrived in New York and Edith called to ask if I would go with her to the cemetery. The two of us went there alone. It was a miserable; rainy day and I remembered the moving painting by Manet in the Metropolitan Museum of a funeral possession, which Ernest and I had once looked at together. Only this time there was no procession. A representative of the funeral parlor took us to the plot where the ground had been opened for the container of ashes, and he left us there to do as we wished. We looked at each other in embarrassed silence. Edith put some trinkets in the ground on top of the container and asked if I could say a prayer. I recited *Kaddish*, and after a few moments, we walked away in the rain.

In going through Ernest's wallet, Edith found a small painting made by him of people praying before the Western Wall in Jerusalem. She had never seen it before and was puzzled that he would have made a painting on a religious subject since he and she were not followers of organized religion. But it seemed significant, a touching insight into a part of Ernest that he had kept to himself. Edith gave the painting to me and I have it framed and hanging in my house. She also gave me a beautiful pocket watch that shows the months, days of the week, and phases of the moon, and has a wonderful chime; it had belonged to Ernest's grandfather and was one of the few heirlooms he treasured. The watch had been in disrepair for years and Ernest had kept it in a drawer. I had the watch fixed and it now hangs on a chain in my bedroom. Every morning I wind the watch, ring the chimes, and think of Ernest.

Edith was a vigorous 58 years old when Ernest died, so there was some hope that she might still succeed in winning recognition for Ernest's theories. But she had to retire at the age of 65, and in 1972 the Creative Therapy Department at Hillside Hospital was abolished. She subsequently became a consultant to several mental institutions and conducted education courses in Creative Therapy at various colleges. Unfortunately, progressive macular degeneration made reading and writing difficult and driving impossible. She started working on a textbook on Creative Therapy based on her voluminous lecture notes and extensive bibliography. She has recently established the Zierer Research and Study Center for Creative Analysis now located in the Irene Gill

Memorial Library of the College of New Rochelle (New York). Its archive includes approximately 15,000 paintings by patients of Hillside Hospital, indexed by patient and preserved in especially designed containers. For each collection of paintings, there is a corresponding file of clinical records.

Copies of all writings, published and unpublished, by both Ernest and Edith Zierer, are also part of the archive which has been created as a resource for undergraduate and graduate students of art therapy engaged in the study of the theory and practice of Creative Analysis.

The Zierer Center officially opened on October 5, 1992, and although Edith's health was failing at the age of 85 and she had become blind, she managed to be present for the occasion. Her face was radiant as the archives were described in a brief presentation, and afterwards she said with a note of triumph, "I made it." She had struggled to live long enough to see the Center established. I also had the proofs of *The Story of Ernest* with me, and she was grateful to know that the book would soon be published. That night Edith suffered a stroke, and on November 1, she died.

Her greatest fear during those last years, which I shared was that Ernest's achievements might ultimately sink into oblivion. All the records and writings that exist do not make up for the deep insight which came from Ernest directly as he explained his theories face to face. She and I were probably the only two remaining people to have been privileged to have worked closely with this enigmatic genius, and we had suffered the frustration all these years of knowing that the world was turning a deaf ear to him.

That is why I have written *The Story of Ernest*. It is

my way of thanking him for opening my eyes and mind to a profound truth and of expressing my undiminished conviction that the Zierer theory reveals an unexplored realm of art and the human personality. My hope is that this brief account will give some intimation of Ernest's extraordinary discoveries, and help future generations have an opportunity to glimpse a revolutionary insight which this generation has ignored.

AFTERWORD

When the first draft of The Story of Ernest *was written, I sent copies to several friends to get their reaction. I was greatly encouraged by the warm responses I received from Norman Cousins, Louis Finkelstein, Meyer Schapiro, Frank Stanton and others, all of whom urged me to have it published. The most enthusiastic response, however, came from my friend John Walsh, publisher of Black Swan Books, who decided to publish the book himself. As the text went through several drafts, John performed his role of careful editor, suggesting that I eliminate sections that distracted from the main story, and helping me to refine descriptions of the subtleties involved in Ernest's theory. As was the case with all his books, every sentence was scrutinized, and I had the satisfaction of knowing that my final words had passed through the screen of his fine mind.*

John died from cancer at the young age of 49 just before the book was printed, and although it may be one of the lesser of his many significant publications, I wanted to dedicate The Story of Ernest *to him as an expression of my deep gratitude for his interest and help.*

SELECTED BIBLIOGRAPHY

Zierer, Ernest. *Kunst und Weltgesetze, Neue Wege Ihrer Erforschung.* Stockholm: Nordiska Boktryckeriet, 1924.

_____. *Erdbuch: Ein Abwicklungsgesetz.* Stockholm: Nordiska Boktryckeriet, 1924.

_____. *Ursprung der Barocken Kuppel.* Stockholm: Research University, 1924.

_____. *An die Künstler.* Stockholm: Nordiska Boltryckeriet, 1927.

_____. *Intuitive Kunst.* Stockholm: Nordiska Boltryckeriet, 1927.

_____. *Objective Wertgruppierung.* Berlin: J.J. Ottens Verlag, 1930.

_____. *Erziehung auf Grundlage der Absoluten Tiefenanschauung.* Berlin: Kunst und Jugend, 1931.

_____. *Kinderzeichnungen und Kunstunterricht.* Berlin: Kunst und Jugend, 1931.

_____. *Neuaufbau der Kunstkritik durch die Absolute Tiefenanschauung.* Überlingen: Verlag Seebote, 1931.

_____. *Objective Wertgruppierung: Kunstmonographische Übersicht uber das Werk des Walter Kurau.* Berlin: J.J. Ottens Verlag, [no date].

_____. *Bipolaridad en la Esquizofrenia.* Translated by Gabriel de la Vega, M.D. Montevideo, *Uruguay: Revista de Psiquiatria del Uruguay*, 1948.

_____. "Dynamics and Diagnostic Value of Creative Therapy, 1: The Body-Space Test." *Acta Medica Orientalia* [Jerusalem], vol. IX, no. 2 (February 1950):1-9.

_____. "Bipolarity in Diagnosis Through Art." *American Journal of Psychotherapy*, vol. IV, no. 3 (July 1950):448-99.

_____. "Dynamics and Diagnostic Value of Creative Therapy, 2: Element Integration." *Acta Medica Orientalia* [Jerusalem], vol. X, no. 2 (February 1951):41-8.

Zeirer, Edith. "Body-Space Test for Adolescents and Adults." *Scoring* [New York], 1951.

_____. "Transference in Creative Therapy." *Journal of the Hillside Hospital* [New York], vol I, no. 2 (April 1952):93-102.

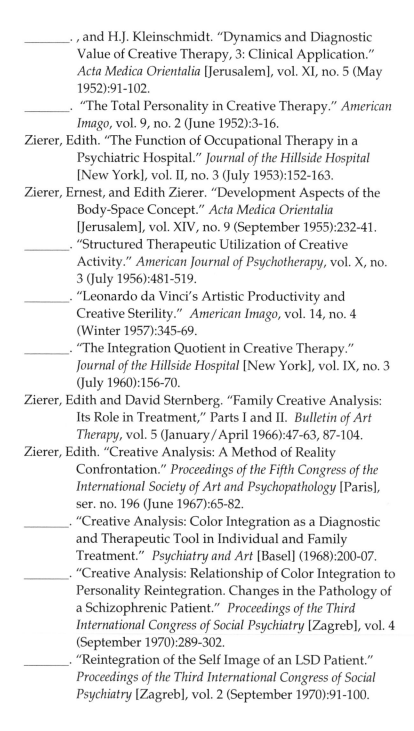

_____. , and H.J. Kleinschmidt. "Dynamics and Diagnostic Value of Creative Therapy, 3: Clinical Application." *Acta Medica Orientalia* [Jerusalem], vol. XI, no. 5 (May 1952):91-102.

_____. "The Total Personality in Creative Therapy." *American Imago*, vol. 9, no. 2 (June 1952):3-16.

Zierer, Edith. "The Function of Occupational Therapy in a Psychiatric Hospital." *Journal of the Hillside Hospital* [New York], vol. II, no. 3 (July 1953):152-163.

Zierer, Ernest, and Edith Zierer. "Development Aspects of the Body-Space Concept." *Acta Medica Orientalia* [Jerusalem], vol. XIV, no. 9 (September 1955):232-41.

_____. "Structured Therapeutic Utilization of Creative Activity." *American Journal of Psychotherapy*, vol. X, no. 3 (July 1956):481-519.

_____. "Leonardo da Vinci's Artistic Productivity and Creative Sterility." *American Imago*, vol. 14, no. 4 (Winter 1957):345-69.

_____. "The Integration Quotient in Creative Therapy." *Journal of the Hillside Hospital* [New York], vol. IX, no. 3 (July 1960):156-70.

Zierer, Edith and David Sternberg. "Family Creative Analysis: Its Role in Treatment," Parts I and II. *Bulletin of Art Therapy*, vol. 5 (January/April 1966):47-63, 87-104.

Zierer, Edith. "Creative Analysis: A Method of Reality Confrontation." *Proceedings of the Fifth Congress of the International Society of Art and Psychopathology* [Paris], ser. no. 196 (June 1967):65-82.

_____. "Creative Analysis: Color Integration as a Diagnostic and Therapeutic Tool in Individual and Family Treatment." *Psychiatry and Art* [Basel] (1968):200-07.

_____. "Creative Analysis: Relationship of Color Integration to Personality Reintegration. Changes in the Pathology of a Schizophrenic Patient." *Proceedings of the Third International Congress of Social Psychiatry* [Zagreb], vol. 4 (September 1970):289-302.

_____. "Reintegration of the Self Image of an LSD Patient." *Proceedings of the Third International Congress of Social Psychiatry* [Zagreb], vol. 2 (September 1970):91-100.

_____. "Reintegration of an LSD Patient." *Psychiatry and Art* [Basel], vol. 3 (1971):184-205.

_____. "Creative Analysis: A Projective Technique and Structured Therapeutic Method." *Art Psychotherapy*, vol. 1, no. 2 (1973): 101-03.

_____. "Case Study: Creative Analysis of a Family." *American Journal of Art Therapy*, vol. 14, no. 2 (1975):49-53.

_____. "Methods of Communication and Levels of Objectives in Creative Analysis." *Psychiatry and Art* [Basel], vol. 4 (1975):270-76.

_____. "Creative Analysis: A Nonverbal and Verbal Psychotherapy Technique." *Art Psychotherapy*, vol. 3, no. 1 (1976):27-41.

_____. "Kreativ Analyse im Rahmen einer Familientherapie." *Handbuch der Psychiatrie*, (1975):271-74.

_____. , Janet Jacobs and Marilyn Moore. "Identification of an Art Therapist through Creative Analysis." *Proceedings of the Seventh Annual Conference of the AATA* [Baltimore, MD], (October 1976):66-9.

_____. "Family Art Therapy Study Session." *Proceedings of the Seventh Conference of the AATA* [Baltimore, MD], (October 1976):26-7.

_____. "The Use of Painting in Family Creative Analysis." *Japanese Bulletin of Art Therapy*, vol. 9 (1978):137-44.

_____. "Getting Older in a Changing Society: Problems and Problem Solving." *Proceedings of the Ninth Annual Conference of the AATA (1978)*. Published in *Art Therapy:Expanding Horizons* (American Art Therapy Association:1978-79) pp. 66-9.

_____. "Another Reaction to Therapeutic Doctrine and the Artist-Client." *American Journal of Art Therapy*, vol. 18 (April 1979).

_____. "Creative Therapy: Gerontology and Geriatrics.: *Bulletin of Expressive Art Therapy for the Elderly*, vol. 1, (Spring-Summer 1981).

Wetzenstein, Ernst. *Kritische Betrachtungen der Ziererschen Kunstkritik.* Berlin:J.J. Ottens Verlag, 1928.

Merwart, Fritz. *Zierers Tiefenanschauung und Ihre erzieherische Bedeutung.* Berlin:Kunst und Jugend, 1928.

Folke, Marell. *Zierers Tiefenanschauung. Drei Essays.* Stockholm, 1933.

Donath, Adolph. *Der Neue Hoffer Ausstellung bei Fleethteim.* 1931.

Silberman, I. "Art in Diagnosis." *Bulletin of the American Psychoanalytic Association of New York* [Washington, DC, 1948], vol. 4, no. 3.

Kleinschmidt, H.J. "Organization and Management of a Progressive Psychiatric Institution." *Acta Medica Orientalia* [Jerusalem], vol. 7, no.7-8 (1948).

Kleinschmidt, H.J. and Jos. S. Miller. "An Early Diagnosis of Schizophrenia." *Acta Medica Orientalia* [Jerusalem], vol. 8, no. 5-6 (1949).